GUN RIGHTS FACT BOOK

Other Books by Alan M. Gottlieb

The Rights of Gun Owners
The Gun Grabbers

GUN RIGHTS FACT BOOK

Alan M. Gottlieb

Distributed By
MERRIL PRESS
PO Box 1682 Bellevue, WA 98009

GUN RIGHTS FACT BOOK

A Merril Press Book/published
by arrangement with the author

Fourth Printing

For information write: Merril Press, P. O. Box 1682,
Bellevue, Washington 98009. Telephone (206)454-7009.

Library of Congress Cataloging-In-Publication Data
Gottlieb, Alan M.
Gun rights fact book/Alan Gottlieb
p. cm.
Bibliography: p.
ISBN 0-936783-03-6 $7.95
1. Firearms—Law and legislation—United States.
2. Firearms owners—legal status, laws, etc.—United
States. 3. Gun Control—United States. I. Title.
KF3941.Z9G67 1988
344.74'0533—dc19
[347.304533]   87-37209
                CIP

Printed in the United States of America

Acknowledgements

I wish to express my tremendous gratitude to the many people in the gun community who made this book possible. John West, Jr. contributed a majority of the back breaking research work upon which most of this book is based. Without him this project would have never been completed.

Joe Friend spent many hours proofing, editing and guiding this book along its way. John Snyder and Joe Tartaro gave me invaluable insights into improving the book, as did many of the participants of the first annual Gun Rights Policy Conference where an early draft of this book first saw light.

Karen Friend helped in the revision of the book from an early manuscript.

And finally, all the gun owners who have called requesting information have contributed greatly. It was their questions that led me to see the need for a book such as this.

Table of Contents

Introduction

He who molds public sentiment goes deeper than
he who enacts statutes or pronounces decisions. He
makes statutes or decisions possible or impossible
to execute.
    — Abraham Lincoln,
        the Lincoln-Douglas Debates

Do you, as a law-abiding gun owner in the United
States, hope to exert meaningful influence on
legislation that affects you? Do you seek to register
your opinion instead of your firearms? Then you must
know how to reach the people who make decisions that
concern your constitutional right to keep and bear arms
before those decisions are made.

When elected officials give serious consideration to
their policy decisions, they usually consider two major
factors: their own moral position and public opinion
within their constituencies. Both factors have weight
on their decisions, but for practical purposes most
elected officials must consider the second more
important. Obviously, they want to be re-elected and
therefore will value the opinions of the voters in their
constituencies.

With increasing frequency the Members of Congress
are called upon to make decisions on legislation and
policy that could infringe on your constitutional right to
own and use firearms. As a gun owner you have an
obligation to be a vocal constituent. The issue is

sensitive but simple. If many of our national leaders are now undecided, persuasive communications from gun owners will play a role in their eventual decisions.

If U.S. political leaders disregard the Constitution and Bill of Rights, silent citizens can only blame themselves. We have optimum opportunity to exercise our influence over the direction of freedom. Unfortunately, it is all too easy to spend time keeping our firearms free from rust while at the same time our liberties are corroding away. Too many gun owners in our country exercise no more political freedom than the ordinary Russian citizen is permitted.

Before you, a responsible gun owner, attempt to exert influence on the political system, however, you must become knowledgeable: learn the facts, understand who your friends are, and know how to reach them. Even if you cannot memorize all the facts and statistics, you need to know where to find them. This book will help you.

First, it will equip you with the weapons you need to influence the political process. Part one of the book discusses five tools that you can use to further the gun rights cause.

Second, the book will arm you with the ammunition you need to fight the gun-banners. Part two gives you detailed facts and information that you can use to counter the lies, half-truths and distortions of the anti-gun groups.

Finally, part three of this book contains reference materials to help you along in your own particular endeavors.

Section I
Political Action

Letters to Congress

As a former member of a congressional staff, I can assure you that writing to Washington, D.C. or your state capitol is not a waste of time. Congressmen pay attention to their mail. They have to because your views help form a major listening post of voter sentiment on pending legislation. A surprising number of letters are read carefully by Congressmen themselves. Those that are not are handled by key staff personnel who notify their bosses of the contents.

Here are some guidelines to keep in mind when writing letters.

If you expect to influence legislation and policies significantly, you should time your communications properly. Obviously you must register your opinion before decisions are made. At the time the Administration is seriously considering a certain anti-gun proposal write to the President or the Attorney General. Write about a gun control bill you are interested in when it is introduced into Congress and assigned to committees. Letters to members of the House and Senate committees may help to get the bill killed without even going to the floor for consideration. Remember that about 90 percent of the bills passed by Congress are adopted in virtually the same form in which they appeared when reported out of committee, so influencing committee action is critical.

Communications are also very effective when a congressional committee holds up proposed pro-gun legislation. Another strategic time to contact your legislator is after a committee reports out a bill and before the House and Senate vote. Be sure you are acquainted with the changes made by the committee. One or two words may alter the entire effect of the bill.

When possible, always refer to the bill under discussion by its name and number. Make reference to specific wording you oppose.

Communication with the chairman of the committee handling a gun control bill is often an effective tool for influencing opinion. Send a carbon copy of your letter to the ranking member of the minority party (who could become chairman if his or her party were to achieve majority status in the future). Don't ignore the chairmen of certain key subcommittees of Congress; the whole committee often gives quick approval to the reports.

Avoid form letters with identical wording. Avoid long telegrams signed by lists of people. These communications do not carry as much weight in Washington as the simplest handwritten letter. The legislators know from experience that sudden outpourings with suspicious similarities come largely from disinterested persons who were goaded into signing a form letter or preprinted postcard by some lobbyist or political action group. Of course, any form of communication is better than nothing at all. The influence of your communication depends upon the point you make and the clarity with which you make it. A carefully thought-out individual letter is the most influential.

The following suggestions for writing to an elected official will make your letters more effective:

- Keep each letter brief. Limit it to a single subject.

- Name the constitutional issues. Specify why you are personally advocating a particular position. If an organization to which you belong has taken an official action on the issue, you may want to refer to that.

- Be courteous. If possible, compliment the legislator on some recent action, vote, or public speech. This is important. Letters to a member of Congress for a job well done are altogether too rare.

- To get a personal response, ask a thoughtful question. Ask for the legislators opinion, or after you have stated your opinion, write, Can I count on your support?

- Address your letters correctly. Here are some examples:

The President:
The President
The White House
1600 Pennsylvania Avenue
Washington, DC 20500

Dear Mr. President:

Members of the Senate:
The Honorable (full name)
United States Senate
Washington, DC 20510

Dear Senator (last name):

Members of the House of Representatives:
The Honorable (full name)
House of Representatives
Washington, DC 20515

Dear Representative (last name):

Members of the Cabinet:
The Honorable (full name)
(correct title such as Attorney General)
(correct department, such as The Department of
Justice)
Washington, DC (zip)

Dear Mr. (last name):

Members of the Judiciary:
The Honorable (full name)
(Title: Chief Justice or Associate Justice)
United States Supreme Court
Washington, DC 20543

Dear Mr. Justice:

Lobbying

In this chapter, I will explain how to lobby government officials through personal contacts and by testifying before governmental bodies. In the text, I will refer specifically to United States Congressmen and Senators. My comments, however, should be read as applying to all of the elected officials who claim to represent you on a local, state, or federal basis.

Visiting Your Congressman

Appointments are relatively easy to arrange. You may visit your Congressman at his office in Washington, D.C. or in the home district office. If you plan the visit during a trip to Washington, remember that Congress conducts most of its major business Tuesday through Thursday. The member will probably be in the office on one of those days.

The best way to make an appointment with the Congressman is by writing to his office. If you represent a local gun club or group of sportsmen, name the group you represent. If you do not personally know the member in question, write to him on your club stationary, tell him about your interest in the issue, and ask for an appointment. When you arrive in Washington, telephone to confirm the meeting time. Remember to:

- Acquaint yourself with the Congressman's voting record.

- Start your interview on a friendly note, even though you may be displeased with the member's political position. Then, turn the discussion to your main issue. If he has been voting for gun controls, for instance, suggest that he may be losing favor with his constituents.

- Limit yourself to one topic. Be well informed. You may want to bring some of your organization's press releases or other documentation that analyzes a specific problem.

- Have a clear idea of what you want the Congressman to do. Which bills should he support? Which should he be against? Advise him. Perhaps you want to introduce a bill. Be definite in your recommendations. Be able to support your position.

- Remember that one of the greatest concerns of your Congressman is reelection. Remind him gently of the support he will receive if he shows genuine concern for sportsmen and gun owners.

- When the meeting is over, thank the Congressman for his time and promise to keep in touch. Leave him with a brief, friendly letter explaining what you wish him to do. This makes it much easier for him to remember what you said and considerably increases the chances he will act favorably. Later, remember to drop him a note expressing your thanks for his time. This will jog his memory and remind him of your requests.

- If you have not already done so, put the Congressman on your mailing list. He should receive all your press releases and position statements.

If you've done all these things, chances are good that you've made a lasting impression on the legislator and that you will be remembered.

Inviting a Congressman to Speak Before Your Group

Many gun clubs meet regularly with their Congressmen and Senators in their home towns. Meetings like these have several advantages. They help develop closer working relationships with elected representatives. They increase the stature of the organization in the community. They stimulate a keener interest in national affairs, and thus perform a public service. Members of Congress usually welcome these meetings. To maintain good relationships with citizens in the communities they represent, they need to know what these constituents are thinking.

Planning the program

A successful meeting with a Congressman or Senator depends upon orderly planning of the program. The best type of program may not revolve around a speech by the guest of honor. A better type of meeting may be one that features a discussion of legislative issues. It is better because it permits an exchange of fact and opinion.

Discussion of issues will contribute greatly to the development of a good working relationship with your elected representative. In order to discuss issues effectively, it is necessary to be specific. The best results are obtained if your meeting is arranged and supervised by persons equipped to conduct a discussion of major questions involved in important legislation.

A well-planned discussion of issues will be evidence of the interest of your community in what your elected representative is doing, and of your intention to "keep tabs" on the way he votes on gun legislation. Most members of Congress will be gratified to witness evidence of interest in the processes of representative government.

Here are some suggestions you may find useful in planning the program for a meet-your-Congressman meeting:

Arrange a meeting with a newly-elected or re-elected Congressman or Senator at a convenient time between the November elections and the opening of Congress in January. Thereafter, set up periodic meetings when your Congressmen and Senators are back home between sessions, or are on "pulse-taking" and "fence-mending" visits during sessions. Congressmen often are home during traditional congressional recess periods: President's Day observances, Easter, Memorial Day, Independence Day, and Labor Day.

Suggest a date, time, and place in a letter of invitation to a congressman or senator, but ask the guest to name an alternative date if he cannot be present on the date mentioned. Make an effort to choose a date, time, and place that will encourage maximum attendance by the members of your organization.

If a legislative action committee is functioning in your group, have the committee chairman send the letter of invitation. The chairman and committee members should then arrange and conduct the meeting.

Agree in advance upon a time limit for the meeting — perhaps a maximum of one hour. Divide the agreed-upon time in such a way as to promote an orderly discussion of issues. Here is a sample schedule:

5 minutes: Introduction of elected official by presiding officer. If the Senator or Congressman wishes to make a brief five to ten minute statement after being introduced, the time should be allotted.

30 minutes: Introduction of presiding officer or person who will ask questions; question-and-answer session with Congressman or Senator.

20 minutes: General discussion of points raised in the question-and-answer session.

5 minutes: Summary and concluding remarks by presiding officer.

Arrange for persons informed on issues to draw up discussion questions in advance of the meeting. Make sure that questions are straightforward and to the point and that they relate to major legislative issues before Congress. Questions should be phrased to reveal your sincere interest in obtaining information about proposed legislation and the opinions of the Senator or Congressman on it. They should not reflect belligerence or antagonism.

Divide questions into categories as an effective way of covering all the points you may want to raise. Furnish the principal questions to your guest in advance.

Arrange for introduction by the presiding officer of persons who will ask the questions. Where a legislative action committee is functioning, a committee member usually is appointed by the chairman.

Conducting the meeting

In conducting a meet-your-Congressman meeting, the presiding officer will find these suggestions useful:

In your brief introductory talk explain the purpose of the meeting and the procedure to be followed.

Make sure that the time limits are observed both in introductory remarks and in question-and-answer periods.

Include in your introduction a certain amount of biographical information about the guest of honor, unless his background already is well known. If the guest has served in Congress for some time, you may want to mention his congressional committee assignments and something of his legislative record. (Biographical data can be obtained from the office of the congressman or senator.) Thank the guest for any of his constructive accomplishments in the community or in Congress that are worthy of special notice.

If you are chairman of a legislative action committee you may want to say a few words about the committee. Introduce committee members who are present. Invite other interested persons to become members of the committee.

Question-and-answer period

After being introduced by the presiding officer, the person designated to ask the questions can make a brief introductory statement that points out the basic issues involved, paying particular attention to the impact of these issues on the local community.

Discussion can be stimulated through one or two basic questions. After the guest of honor has answered and commented on these questions, the audience can be invited to ask supplementary questions.

This process can be repeated for additional questions if the discussion of the first one or two questions does not consume the scheduled time.

The person presenting the questions should take care to make them clear and to bring out their full implications. Greater interest will be stimulated if persons in the audience can relate the questions under discussion to their own interests or to those of the community.

General discussion

At the conclusion of the question-and-answer period, your guest of honor and the audience may want to discuss some points further. For this reason, a concluding general session or catch-all period usually is advisable. Under a logical division of time for a meeting lasting one hour, twenty minutes could be set aside for this period.

In brief concluding remarks, the presiding officer should summarize the main points brought out in the discussion.

Dealing with press representatives

A meeting at which a Congressman or Senator appears is usually covered by the press, particularly a meeting at which issues are discussed. What the elected representative may say about issues will be news. Therefore, when planning a meeting with a Congressman or Senator, notify representatives of local newspaper and radio and television stations of the date, time, and place of the meeting.

This is best accomplished by a press release giving details about the meeting and informing press representatives that they will be welcome. In many instances, it may be desirable to include in the press release biographical data about a visiting Congressman or Senator. (See sample press release below. Also see discussion of press releases in the third chapter of this section.)

A press table or reserved seats should be set aside for the press representatives at a place in the meeting hall where they can hear, so that they can report accurately what is said.

Occasionally, a visiting official may want to hold a press conference in connection with the meeting. Perhaps the press representatives want to arrange a conference with the visitor. This can be worked out on the spot or through communication with the Congressman or Senator before the meeting. If a press conference is held, it is better to have it after your meeting when the discussion that has taken place during the question-and-answer session is fresh in the minds of press representatives.

NEWS RELEASE
Citizens Committee for the
Right to Keep and Bear Arms

LIBERTY PARK, 12500 N.E. TENTH PLACE
BELLEVUE, WASHINGTON 98005
(206) 454-4911

*"... the right
of the people to
keep and bear
Arms, shall not
be infringed."*

Contact: ALAN GOTTLIEB, (206) 454-4911

Release: FEBRUARY 31, 2000

CONGRESSMAN PISTOL TO DISCUSS GUN LEGISLATION

BELLEVUE, WASHINGTON -- Congressman Pete Pistol, of (place of
residence), will discuss gun control legislation currently before
Congress at a meeting of the (name of organization) on (date).

The meeting will be held at 7:30 p.m. in the Hometown Hall, Mr.
Winchester, Chairman of the Legislative Action Committee, is in
charge of the meeting program and will preside.

Mr. Pistol has agreed to answer questions about major issues
which will be considered by Congress. The questions will relate to
legislation of interest to sportsmen and gun owners.

At this point in the press release, you may want to identify
some of the specific issues that will be discussed. You may want
to mention, in particular, issues coming up for discussion that are
of widespread general interest, and those of greatest interest to
the citizens of your community.

Mr. Pistol represents the (number) District in the House of
Representatives. Include biographical data.

# # # # # #

At the meeting you should furnish the press representatives with prepared copies of the main questions that will form the basis of the discussion. Copies of any prepared statements made at the meeting may be given to the press representatives at the conclusion of the meeting.

Sample press release and letter of invitation

Figure 1 is an example of a press release that may be issued to local news media after a date has been set for the meeting. While the example relates to a meeting arranged by a legislative action committee with a Congressman-elect, it may be used with appropriate variations for meetings with elected officials generally.

Figure 2 is an example of a letter inviting the guest to attend your meeting. It should be written on the club's official stationary.

How to Testify before Legislative Bodies

Testifying before state legislatures, city councils, and other legislative units is extremely important. Elected officials use this testimony to gauge public opinion and to gain facts to make informed choices on pieces of legislation before them.

To testify on a bill being considered, all you need to do is write a letter or call the appropriate individual to arrange for a date and time. Your local Congressman, state legislator, or city councilman can help you. You can testify as an individual, or member of a club or organization.

It is a good idea to inform your local television stations and home-town newspapers of the date and time you will present your pro-gun rights views and provide them, as well as the members of the body you testify before with a copy of the text of your remarks. This will usually provide a double bonus.

Senator Pete Pistol
Senate Office Building
Washington DC 20510

Dear Senator Pistol:

The Legislative Action Committee of the Hometown
Rifle and Pistol Club would like to have you meet
with us and other interested members of our
organization to discuss the major issues facing
Congress and the nation.

If you can arrange to be with us at (time) on
(date) at (place), we shall set up a meeting for that
time. If this date is not suitable, please suggest an
alternative date.

In addition to informing themselves on
legislative proposals, our committee members have
accepted the task of expressing knowledgeable views
on issues in communications to members of Congress.
Our purpose is to keep tabs on issues that are of
vital importance to our community, sportsmen, and gun
owners.

We would be interested in having your views on
conservation, gun control, and crime control issues
likely to arise in Congress.

To conserve time and yet cover all categories, we
want to limit the meeting to about one hour.

Our plan is to allot thirty minutes to a
discussion and about thirty minutes to questions, or
one hour in all. One of our committee members will
present the questions.

We intend to prepare several important questions
in advance of the meeting, and if you wish we will be
glad to send copies of them to you so that you may be
thinking about them.

Because of widespread interest in what you may
have to say, we plan to invite our local newspaper
and radio and TV press to cover the meeting.

I sincerely hope that you can arrange to be with
us.

        Cordially,
        Harry Winchester
        Chairman, Legislative Action Committee

FIGURE 2

The following is an example that you can pattern your statement after:

Statement of
John M. Snyder
Director of Publications and Public Affairs
Citizens Committee for the Right to Keep and Bear
Arms
Before the
Subcommittee on the Constitution
Committee on the Judiciary
United States Senate
Washington, D.C.

Mr. Chairman and Members of the Subcommittee:

Let me express my thanks for this opportunity to testify during this public hearing on S. 466, a bill to mandate a national waiting period before the sale, delivery or transfer of a handgun.

We oppose this bill for several reasons.

First of all, a waiting period undercuts the right to self-defense and, therefore, the right to life itself.

If the life of a single innocent person is snuffed out through criminal violence because that innocent was unable to obtain a handgun with which to defend himself or herself against criminal attack as the result of a handgun purchase waiting period requirement, the blood of that innocent person will be on the hands and consciences of the promoters of such waiting period requirement for the rest of their lives.

While it is not known precisely how many times the inability of a law-abiding citizen to obtain one quickly would result in victimization by murder, it is known that, according to a 1978 survey conducted by Cambridge Reports, Inc. for the Center for the Study and Prevention of Handgun Violence, "three percent of the population has actually used a handgun for self-defense." That comes out, roughly, to over six million people. Have the perpetrators of the handgun purchase waiting period requirement even begun to contemplate the millions of lives which, conceivably, could be jeopardized by this proposal?

We also oppose S. 466 because we think it could provide a legal basis for incipient, partial, national handgun registration. While the bill does provide for destruction of sworn statements relating to prospective handgun transactions, it does not provide for destruction of the information contained in such statements. Conceivably, then, this information could be retained in local police records and transferred, subsequently, to a national handgun registry. If there is anything America's tens of millions of law-abiding firearms owners as a group most assuredly will oppose, it is national gun registration. It should be clear, therefore, that this bill, ultimately, will meet with the opposition, substantially, of 80 million law-abiding American citizen gun owners. When one considers that this is more people than vote for both major party presidential candidates every four years, one may begin to get some idea of the massive public opposition with which this bill, potentially is faced.

While the bill, if enacted into law, would undermine the legitimate interests of law-abiding citizens, it would have little, if any effect in furthering its stated purpose, a reduction in criminal violence perpetrated with the use of handguns.

According to the July, 1985 U.S. Department of Justice research report prepared for the National Institute of Justice on "The Armed Criminal In America, A Survey of Convicted Felons" by James D. Wright and Peter H. Rossi, only 21 percent of felons' handguns are obtained through retail channels. The rest, 79 percent, are obtained from family and friends, various gray and black market sources and a variety of other sources. To maintain that a person intent on committing a crime of violence would subject himself to the checks associated with a handgun purchase waiting period requirement is an incredible position. The bill, in other words, while it might be effective in undermining the legitimate interests of law-abiding citizens, would be ineffective in undermining the nefarious interests of violent criminals.

While proponents of the waiting period concept maintain it would reduce "crimes of passion," the fact of the matter is that most "crimes of passion" occur between the hours of 10 p.m. and 3 a.m., when gun shops aren't open anyway, suggesting that the immediate availability of handguns over the counter really is not a factor in such killings.

The argument that a waiting period will create a delay while it can be determined if the buyer has a criminal record or otherwise is disqualified legally from owning a handgun also is of dubious merit.

The handgun owner licensing provisions under New York State law indicate the futility of waiting periods as crime prevention measures. The State's handgun purchasing process amounts to the most comprehensive of background checks and the longest of waiting periods, commonly one or two years for first time handgun buyers despite State law requiring action within six months. However, New York State has one of the higher crime and illegal gun ownership rates.

That criminals don't abide by waiting period provisions or other firearms-related provisions is evident also from the same Justice Department study referred to earlier in this testimony. According to it, felons, who, under Federal law are not allowed to acquire or own firearms, were asked how long it would take them, upon release from prison, to obtain the handgun they wanted. According to the report, "nearly 80 percent of the sample said they could get a handgun in a few days or less; among the Predators, the figure rose to about 90 percent. Over half the predators said they could arm themselves in a few hours."

A mandated national handgun purchase waiting period, then, really would not have a positive impact on crime. It might, however, have a negative impact by telling the elderly, city residents, women and others who most frequently are victims of violent crime that they must wait a long time before they can purchase a handgun with which to defend themselves, thus letting them know that now they are going to be even more helpless and supine before the criminal element than they were before the waiting period law.

In fact, a waiting period requirement could be even more burdensome for law-abiding citizens than a licensing requirement. Whereas a licensing system requires approval for each individual purchase. When one considers that tens of millions of law-abiding handgun owners would oppose, adamantly, a national handgun owner licensing law, one can imagine how much more adamantly opposed those tens of millions of voters would be to a national purchase waiting period requirement.

When one considers, also, that there have been times when agencies, so overloaded with paperwork, have had to suspend firearm forms processing, and that this kind of eventuality could occur under the proposed system, one can see another reason for general opposition to the proposal.

Section 2. (a)(p)(1)(B) of S. 466, relating to the issuance of a certificate from the chief law enforcement officer of the place of residence of the transferee to the transferor regarding requisite access to a handgun because of a threat to the life of the transferee, since it contains no clear statement regarding the cause for the issuance of such a certificate, crates the possibility for capricious issuance of such certificates.

This provision could be used by a local racist officer, for instance, to arm all members of one racial group to the detriment of members of another racial group. It is, in other words, a potentially very dangerous provision.

Despite the support S. 466 has received from spokesmen for some organizations of law enforcement officers, its enactment would not necessarily be the boon to law enforcement professionals its supporters claim. One thing about it which disturbs Gerald S. Arenberg, Executive Director of the National Association of Chiefs of Police, is that it might create possible tortious liability for chief law enforcement officers of the places of residence of transferees if such transferees victimize individuals subsequent to apparently legitimate handgun acquisition. In addition, Director Arenberg informs me that the NACP currently is polling officers via the mail regarding their opinion of S. 466. It would seem that it would be premature to conclude that S. 466 has the general support of law enforcement before completion of this poll.

Public Relations

Gun owners and supporters of the Second Amendment are bombarded daily with biased and slanted news reporting by the nations press. While the power of any single individual to change these conditions is very weak before the might of TV and newspaper giants, gun rights supporters have seven major ways to make their views and voices of protest heard.

- Communicate through news releases to community newspapers.
- Write frequent letters to the editor.
- Contact local radio and TV stations in order to offer rebuttals to anti-gun editorials or to appear on public affairs talk shows.
- Alert national pro-gun rights groups about significant errors in news reports.
- Complain to the Federal Communications Commission about unfairness in broadcast news.
- Boycott companies that sponsor anti-gun shows.
- Stage a demonstration to oppose anti-gun laws being voted on by local legislative bodies.

In this chapter we will discuss the many ways you and your organization can use public relations tools to tell the pro-gun story.

Public Relations in the Community

A broad variety of activities parade under the banner of public relations. Gun owners must use PR too use it properly as a planned effort to influence public opinion. Only then can we build a favorable public image of those who support our right as law-abiding citizens to keep and bear arms. Our intent should not be to shock or denounce, but to educate and persuade.

In our goal of developing good press relations we ought to be concerned not only with the image of gun owners, but also with the political and moral image of the pro-gun cause. The public opinion on firearms depends upon the image projected for it by the news media. This image has been distorted so far that gun owners are seen as the bogey men of the century.

We must begin the task of improving this image now. We must persuade the press to project the facts about gun rights in America to the public. The way to accomplish this is to present the true image to the press; to take care that the words we write and the activities in which we participate are above reproach at all times; and to see that these works and these writings are so ideally American they cannot be distorted in any way without showing those who distort them to be false and unrealistic.

The Community Newspaper

It has been said that it is in the community that national opinions are formed. If this is so then the community newspaper must have some influence upon the voters. By undertaking the public relations mission within our individual communities across the nation we will be working in an area that has never been fully tapped.

All activities that gun clubs participate in within the community are news. This is the kind of local news that the community paper seeks. You can effectively put the paper to work for you by making use of the unlimited opportunities it offers.

Sometimes called one of the healthiest members of the mass media, the community newspaper family is comprised of over 9,000 weeklies across the nation. Add to this several thousand semi-weekly papers and the community advertisers, and the total would be somewhere around 15,000 papers in this family. These are a great addition to your daily newspaper and radio and TV stations. These 15,000 sources can be put to work to our advantage if they are properly used.

Every American community has one or more newspapers that fall into the weekly category. These papers are primarily concerned with local news, but they sometimes print items of national interest. These papers are an essential part of the community. As a medium of persuasion they are extremely valuable to us. Your community newspaper offers free space for your forum; it reaches all members of the community. There are several such papers in each area, therefore your message will be seen and read several times. This repetition is at the heart of the art of persuasion.

The result will be not just to gain publicity for its own sake but to build press relations that can be put to use during campaigns of community, city, state, and national importance during the coming years.

Writing a News Release

News is not restricted to items concerning what has happened and what is going to happen, but also how people think and what they are thinking about. Summed up, newsworthiness consists of reader interest, timeliness, importance, size, newspaper policy, and amount of space available after advertising. As harsh as that last may sound, it is one of the most important reasons for using or omitting your release.

Lets face it, that little piece of literary genius you may have labored for hours over is generally just a piece of filler to the busy editor. If we learn to present our story with color; if we learn to write stories that can capture reader attention; and if we follow the format that will make the editors job easier only then will we have a fair chance of seeing our story in print.

Structure

The three basic news story techniques in wide use today are the fact story, the action story, and the quote story. In the fact story the writer builds his story structure in inverted pyramid style: beginning with the most important fact in the first paragraph, he builds down in order of importance. In the action story the incident or occasion is briefly summarized in the lead. By a retelling process the author adds more detail with each paragraph. In the quote story the lead sentence serves to summarize the story, the second paragraph quotes from the source, and the third leads into further quotes or summarizes a secondary fact. The quote story is used when statements sent from other sources are restated and rewritten. This type of story is covered in more detail later in this chapter.

Leads, Links, and Headlines

In creative writing the writer builds toward a climax. The opposite rule is applied to news writing. In news writing we begin with the climax and work down. Journalists call this structure the inverted pyramid. The first paragraph, the lead, generally contains one or more of the journalists 5 Ws Who? What? When? Where? and Why? These 5 Ws constitute the facts. Try to answer them all in your story.

To link your lead to the body of your story, just fill in the identifications that were too detailed for the lead. You can quote from one of the statements made by the subject of your story. You can explain why if you have not already done so in your lead. Or you can briefly summarize and restate the lead.

Your headline can help to ensure publication of your release or it can cause the story to end in the wastebasket. Although newspapers generally will not use the headline you provide, but will rewrite to suit their style, the headline is important. It tells at a glance the story you are presenting or at least it should tell the story.

The headline should be limited to between five and eight short words. It should arrest attention, it should reflect the content of the story, and it should help the editor judge the story newsworthiness.

Your headline should always be in sentence form, eliminating nonessential articles and conjunctions. Every headline should have a verb, and present tense should always be used.

Always write your story first, then develop the headline. For examples of headline ideas, consult your daily newspaper launch a personal head hunt and make note of suitable ideas.

Format and Style for Submission

Remember your 5 Ws in the preparation of news for dissemination to newspapers, radio, and TV. The same questions must be answered: Who? What? Where? When? Why? and How? if relevant.

A standard format is used for such releases. Following this format you improve your chances of being published. Figure 3 is a good example of a current news release.

- Use a typewriter or word processor.
- Double or triple space between lines.
- Use only one side of the paper.

- Leave 11/2-inch margin on the left side and at the top of the page, and keep your right and bottom margins to at least one inch.

- Indent your paragraphs 5 to 10 spaces.

- Use standard 8 1/2 x 11-inch white or yellow paper (8 1/2 x 14 is sometimes acceptable).

- Number your pages and always type the word more on the bottom of all continuing pages.

- Include the name, address, and telephone number of your groups publicity chairman or other contact in the upper right or left corner of the first page.

- Type an identifying mark on the top of all continuing pages so the editor will know where they belong.

- Date your release. Either give a For Release line flush left over your headline, or type a dateline at the beginning of your first paragraph.

- Use understandable grammar. You only add confusion by using little-known words.

- Do not break a word at the end of a line; if you do not have enough space to complete the word, write it on the next line.

The Managing Editor

The standard format is extremely important in PR operations. A trip through the editorial offices of a newspaper would show you immediately the need for such rules. If you could sit in the slot and work with the copy editors, or sit at the copy desk for a few hours, you'd surely be enlightened. But since this is impossible, lets take an imaginative journey into the editors world. Maybe this particular editor is exaggerated, but then perhaps he may be typical.

His name is Joe Smith and he is managing editor of a small community daily newspaper with an editorial staff of three men and one woman. Each of the members of his staff is delegated different departments in the paper in addition to their responsibilities for reviewing copy, but the bulk of the work and the decisions are Joe's.

Joe is on the receiving end daily of about 20 to perhaps 50 news stories, wire service stories, staff-written stories, and releases from outside sources. It is Joe's job to fill the paper with important and interesting news. It is his job to sort out the newsworthy from the unusable, and it is his job to make up the dummy pages and decide where to put what. Its a big job, and a tiring one.

Joe's desk is in what they call a slot located in the center of a U made up of the desks of the copy people or department writers who work for him. As Joe weeds out the newsworthy releases, he gives them to the copy people to edit, cut, write headlines, or mark up for typesetting.

That inch and a half margin you left on the left side and up at the top above your headline comes in handy here the space at the top is used for a rewrite of your headline or the writing of a new one, for mark up of type size, and so forth.

The space at the side is used to mark up the body of the copy for the size and type of print. The space you left between the lines is used for his editing marks and any rewriting he might do. If you left that space, you are helping him and yourself in the long run.

How does Joe tell what is newsworthy and what is unusable? One good way is to spot read, and I imagine most managing editors are pretty proficient at this. What would he spot? Your headline and your lead! They should tell him what the story is about and help him to judge its newsworthiness. If they don't do that your release will probably end up in the wastebasket. If the release is single-spaced or illegibly handwritten, Joe may not have time to try to decode or strain his eyes to find out if it is usable. It will go into the wastebasket.

So you can see that the format of your release is vital. If you follow the newswriting style facts first the job of the editor and the copy men is made easier. If they have only a little space to fill, they can simply cut out your last paragraph or two and still be certain they have the important facts.

The sample in Figure 3 is presented here to show a release written correctly in standard format.

The Photo Story

Generally newspapers never have enough photographs. Community newspapers face this dilemma more often than the metropolitan dailies which usually have a photo morgue available. You can be fairly certain that a photo story will be used, providing the photo is a good one and the story is of interest.

Many times, for want of a story, PR people will create a photo story around a photograph of some event or person. This story is usually submitted in the form of a brief one-paragraph summary of the pictured activity or person.

When submitting your photo story there are several rules to keep in mind: (1) always lightly write in pencil the subject of the photo and the source on the back of the picture; (2) tape your caption (summary) at the bottom of the photo, applying the tape to the back of the picture; (3) don't clutter your photo with a great number of subjects. If you are picturing people, keep the number to five or less, and show them doing something; (4) submit pictures in black and white, 5 x 6-inch, 7 x 9-inch or 8 x 10-inch.

The AP Stylebook stresses the following for Teletype photo stories which can be readily applied to your captions: Captions must be accurate and complete enough to answer questions a thousand miles away. Captions should be complete enough to stand with the picture without having to lean on a news story for essentials....First names, titles, and identifications are basic. Nicknames should be avoided except for widely known figures.

If the event is of broad interest, call your local papers, news services, and radio and TV stations alerting them in advance; in many cases they will send a photographer to cover the event.

News Services and Radio-TV News Announcements

In addition to the well-known news services such as Associated Press and United Press International, every major city in America has one or more local news service. Addresses can be obtained from your City Chamber of Commerce. When your story has citywide, statewide, or nationwide appeal it is a good idea to send copies of the release to all these services.

As with news services, radio and TV announcers should also be sent releases of news that will appeal to a broader for the addresses and phone numbers of your local radio and TV stations.

Note: When you are planning a gun show or special project phone your local news services and radio and TV stations in advance of the event and on the day on which the event will take place. Have copies of a prepared statement available for newsmen.

Letters to the Editor

Sometimes as important as news releases is the writing of letters to local newspapers. In this area you are free to express yourself without the restrictions set in the newswriting field. Always double space your letters and leave the same margin you allow in your releases. Letters to the editor are marked up in the same manner as news stories.

Don't restrict your mailing of letters to your city dailies only; if you can afford it, send them to all the major metropolitan papers across the state or the nation. You can get the addresses of national metropolitan papers in the Literary Market Place at your local library. If your library does not have this reference book, ask the librarian if they have a newspaper directory for all U.S. cities.

Your city and state Chambers of Commerce provide many services; one you can take immediate advantage of is the publication of a newspaper directory. Almost every Chamber of Commerce makes these directories available to the public for a fee ranging from three to ten dollars. The directory provides the names, addresses, and frequency of publication of each paper. The city directory generally lists all daily and weekly publications in and near the city. If your local Chamber of Commerce does not issue these directories, they can usually refer you to a source.

When you write your letter to the editor, make it brief, to the point, timely, and conciliatory. Finally, identify yourself.

Brief

Most letters should be no more than 200 to 300 words, as space is limited. You will be sharing the Letters to the Editor column with other correspondents on a variety of subjects. Most likely, yours will be triggered by a recent news story or editorial, and it is not necessary to restate the entire premise before launching your views. Of course, limit the subject of your letter to just one topic, news story, or editorial; make your points quickly and cogently.

Pointed

If you don't have pointed, well-developed, firm opinions on an issue, don't bother to write. Editors and their readers enjoy and react to a letter that has fact, feeling, and direction. Unless you have something positive to suggest or correct, something informative and useful for the readers, your letter will accomplish little. Be direct, to the point, and above all, be sure of your facts.

Timely

First impressions are the strongest, and so is the first impact of the news. If the original news story is erroneous or misleading, corrections should be made immediately. Readers are apt to digest the fallacy if the facts come too late. How often have you heard, Of course its true, I read it in the paper just this morning. Editors give priority to letters commenting on a story while it is still news; next week may be too late. Write your letter the same day you read or hear the editorial or news story.

Conciliatory

Even though a news story or editorial may malign one of your pet programs or seem unduly opinionated, do not respond with a sarcastic combative letter. Emotionally charged letters get high readership but at the expense of the writers embarrassment when he sees his hot temper in cold print. If the editorial writer or reporter has been unreasonably critical, point out his errors as factually and politely as possible, correct or amend them, and extend the offer of your services or more information if desired. Above all, you cant intimidate an editor by threatening to cancel your subscription; torrid letters only help increase his circulation. On the other hand, don't feel that an untruth is too gross to be dignified by an answer; silence is sometimes the severest indictment, and an unchallenged fallacy always carries more weight with those who wish to believe it.

Identified

Always sign your letter with your full name and address; add your professional title if it is pertinent to the subject. Anonymous letters lack courage and conviction, and editors seldom print them. Letters with pseudonyms are usually discarded because editors check on the authenticity of both content and correspondent; however, your name may be withheld upon request if circumstances warrant, but these occasions are rare. Do not ask the editor to reply to your letter or to return your manuscript.

Address your letter:

Letters to the Editor
Name of the newspaper or magazine
City, State

Dear Sir:

or

Mr. John S. Doe
Managing Editor
Name of Magazine
Address

Dear Mr. Doe

Meeting the Hostile Newspaper Editor

Although we as gun owners tend to favor those papers that favor us, it would be detrimental to our cause for us to channel all of our efforts into just these favored few. We spend too much time talking to each other and not enough time talking to those who are not in our group. We must reach those of opposing views in order to build our ranks. We must reach those indecisive many whom we laughingly dub fence sitters, for those fence sitters comprise some 60 percent of the voting population.

We must concentrate on all outlets, especially the anti-gun newspaper. Most assuredly we will run into obstacles; but sportsmen naturally thrive on challenge. Certainly there will be editors who will ignore our releases but we must keep sending them if we ever hope to break them down.

One method which is sometimes successful (and should be encouraged) is to hand deliver the releases to the editor. Ask him for advice: How can I improve my releases? What am I doing wrong in my presentation? Since I'm new at this sort of thing, I would be very grateful for any advice you can offer, and so on.

He'd have to be a real stinker not to give you some suggestions. Of course, since he doesn't approve of our philosophy, he might give you a little advice like, Yeah, why don't you join the Coalition to Ban Handguns. But chances are he will bend a little. He will probably give you a little space now and then and you'll reach his readership. They are the kind of people you want to reach.

Dealing with Radio and Television

While newspapers are extremely important, the pro-gun activist should not forget broadcast media outlets. Today most people get their first exposure to a news story from radio or television, not from the newspaper. Indeed, according to some studies, the majority of Americans now get most of their information about outside events from radio and television .

Thus, it is critical that we try to get our message out through radio and television, as well as through newspapers.

Remember, television and radio news is geared to sight and sound. This fact must be recognized by those trying to get coverage of issues they are concerned about. Whereas a newspaper lets you read about an event, a television or radio station wants to let you see and hear it. Thus, broadcast reporters are always looking for stories that will look and sound interesting.

Perhaps this is the reason that a staple of the television news is the demonstration. Television stations in particular love to carry pictures of people carrying placards, chanting, or forming human chains. Broadcast reporters regularly give news time even to the most insignificant groups if the demonstrations they hold are dramatic enough.

How to Conduct a
Successful Demonstration

The first thing to realize is that the demonstration is an art form. Despite how it may look to the television viewer, it is not a spontaneous outpouring of sentiment. You are the one in control. You are responsible for planning out beforehand what will happen and believe me, a demonstration must be planned out as carefully as a stage play.

When to use a demonstration

Demonstrations should be used sparingly, or else the newsmedia will stop covering the ones put on by your group. Demonstrations are particularly appropriate when anti-gun legislation is about to be voted on, or has just been passed.

The most common form of demonstration is picketing. To protest a local gun ordinance, for example, you could round up twenty or thirty people to picket in front of city hall. Another form of demonstration is to hold some sort of ceremony again, in front of city hall or on the capitols steps. The greater the number of people you can say will be there, the more likely the newsmedia will cover the event. Nevertheless, a successful demonstration can be carried off with less than ten people.

Be Creative

Editors and reporters get tired of covering different groups conducting the same sort of demonstrations. So try to be different.

For example, say your city council enacts a handgun ban. Right after the vote your group could stage a mock-burning of the Bill of Rights. Someone could give a short speech emphasizing the importance of the Second Amendment to the Founding Fathers and pointing out how the city council was ignoring this cherished guarantee by voting on the gun ban. In essence, the speaker might declare,the city council has voted to destroy the Bill of Rights. We burn this copy of the Bill of Rights in observance of the shameful deed that the council did this day. After that comment, someone could take a match to a copy of the Bill of Rights. As the document burned, a dramatic visual message would be delivered: the city council has attacked the Bill of Rights by restricting gun rights.

Inviting the Media

To get the newsmedia to cover a demonstration, first send out a press release several days beforehand. Then the day before or day of the event call the city desk of broadcast stations and inform one of the editors personally. If the event is held on short notice, contacting the editors by phone is sufficient.

Caution: It is important that your demonstration be visual, but not emotional. Statements or chants should be non-inflammatory. You want to get the television or radio stations attention, not their contempt. Furthermore, if your demonstration is in a public place, you may need a demonstration permit. Contact your local police department for more information.

Rebuttals of Anti-Gun
Broadcast Editorials

Many TV and radio stations air editorials. Monitor these and if an anti-gun piece appears, be ready to respond. Contact your local TV or radio stations in person or by phone or letters. Stations are obliged to give air time to responsible individuals who disagree with editorials broadcast by the station. It is also wise to contact local radio and TV outlets even when you have an objection to a network show. The networks try to keep their affiliates happy, so they often pay heed to local station reports of audience reaction.

Boycotts of Sponsors

Write sponsors of shows you believed biased or unfair. Commercial advertisers avoid controversy like the plague. If they believe they are losing buyers because they are sponsoring a program, they will back away quickly and the network may reconsider program contents.When writing such a letter to an advertiser, state in courteous but firm language that you will not buy their product as long as the company sponsors that show. Even a handful of such letters, if they are spontaneous and unorganized, can be extremely effective.

Complaints to the
Federal Communications Commission

Complain to the FCC about unfairness in broadcast news. Whatever you feel about the validity of the commissions power, it exists, and it continues to hound stations for lack of programming balance. Licenses of anti-gun stations can be revoked if the offenses are considered grievous. Write to the Federal Communications Commission at 1919 M Street N.W., Washington, DC 20554. The phone number is (202) 632-6600.

Letters to the Networks

Listed below are the addresses, telephone numbers and names of the chief staff members of the major television and radio networks. Direct your calls and letters to specific individuals, if possible. It is also important that you let the local stations know when you are dissatisfied by biased or distorted coverage on television or radio. The networks depend on local outlets and enough complaints from affiliates will have a definite effect on network policy.

American Broadcasting Company (ABC)
1330 Avenue of the Americas
New York, NY 10019
(212) 581-7777

Leonard Goldstein, Chairman of the Board, Capital Cities/ABC Inc.
Daniel Burke, President, Capital Cities/ABC Inc.
Roone Arledge, President, ABC News and Sports
Ben Hoberman, President, ABC Radio
John Severino, President, ABC Television
James Duffy, President, ABC Television Network
Lewis H. Erlicht, President, ABC Entertainment
Robert E. Frye, Executive Producer, ABC World News Tonight

Columbia Broadcasting System (CBS)
51 W. 52nd St.
New York, NY 10019
(212) 765-4321

Thomas H. Wyman, Chairman of the Board
Gene Jankowski, President, CBS Broadcasting Group
Anthony C. Malara, President, CBS Television Network
Robert L. Hosking, President, CBS Radio Division
Edward Joyce, President, CBS News Division
John Lane, Vice President and Director, CBS News
B. Donald Grant, President, CBS Entertainment Division
Howard Stinger with Dan Rather, Executive Producer, CBS Evening News

National Broadcasting Company (NBC)
30 Rockefeller Plaza
New York, NY 10020
(212) 664-4444

Robert Wright, Chairman NBC-TV
Robert E. Mulholland, President, NBC Network
Lawrence Frank, President, NBC News
Pierson Mapes, President, NBC Television
Brandon Tartikoff, President, NBC Entertainment
Paul Greenburg, Executive Producer, NBC Nightly News
Mike Eskridge, President, NBC Radio

Cable News Network (CNN)
1050 Techwood Drive, N.W.
Atlanta, Georgia 30318
(404) 827-1500

Ted Turner, Chairman of the Board, Turner Broadcasting System
Burt Reinhardt, President, Cable News Network Headline Service

Public Broadcasting Service (PBS)
475 LEnfant Plaza S.W.
Washington, D.C. 20024
(202) 488-5276

Bruce L. Christensen, President

National Public Radio
2025 M St. N.W.
Washington, D.C. 20036
(202) 822-2010

Douglas J. Bennet, President

Corporation for Public Broadcasting
111 16th Street N.W.
Washington, D.C. 20036
(202) 955-5275

Martin Rubenstein, President

Cable Satellite Public Affairs Network (C-SPAN)
Suite 155, 400 N. Capitol Street, N.W.
Washington, D.C. 20001
(202) 737-3220

Ed Allen, Chairman of the Board
Brian P. Lamb, President

Alerting Pro-Gun Groups

If you discover a significant factual error in a news report, inform the Citizens Committee for the Right to Keep and Bear Arms or the National Rifle Association immediately. The Citizens Committee monitors gun news reporting practices and, on occasion, launches embarrassing lawsuits to keep networks and journals of all kinds honest. The Committee also corrects the record by publishing the names of offending reporters accompanied by a factual account of the story.

Conclusion

As with all professions that deal with the public, many written and unwritten rules of ethics apply to organizations and individuals in fields like ours. In the next few pages I will try to summarize briefly those codes I feel are applicable in our work.

To begin with, in order to persuade the media to present an honest image of our ideals, we must show honesty and sincerity in our relations with the press and the public.

Like all humans, we too err, and certainly we will continue to err now and then. But as public relations people, we must always keep the best interest in mind. Our manners will reflect upon all gun owners. Our ability and trustworthiness as private citizens will reflect upon the ability and trustworthiness of us all. Our actions will be judged as the actions of the gun rights cause. Our faults will be used against us, but our good deeds and good manners will serve to eradicate the false image painted by the opposition.

This is even more true in our work as newswriters. If malice shows in our writing, if we constantly attack individuals and organizations, if we falsely accuse and malign other organizations or individuals then we defeat our goal, and rather than draw sympathetic observers into our ranks we will frighten them away. Further, we will most certainly turn even more members of the media against our side.

We are the only side of gun owners the editor sees, therefore we truthfully do represent our organization. If we keep this in mind, we will need no code of ethics other than the ideals and philosophy set forth in the Second Amendment combined with our own honesty and sincerity.

When registering disapproval, present your facts with honesty, never with malice; use facts, not suppositions. This is the best way to tear down the facade of democracy the gun ownership opponents hide behind.

If our facts are presented clearly they cannot be easily misinterpreted. If the facts are misinterpreted, abusing the editor or broadcaster will not help the truth. Instead we must approach him with the clear facts and request that they be brought to the attention of his readers.

Remember, if the editor or broadcaster knows us personally, he will think more than twice before he twists anything we say or write. Our first job is to meet the editor, get to know him or her, and present ourselves as law-abiding gun owners, a respected and respectful group in the community.

This is the only way we will ever achieve our goals.

Public Speaking and Debating

In trying to influence public opinion, what you know is sometimes less important than how you present it. Vocal presentations must be smooth, logical, and backed up with facts if they are to be truly effective. This chapter contains information that can help make your spoken messages effective no matter what form they take. Here you will find pointers on how to give a speech, how to debate an opponent, how to speak on television, and how to prepare for a radio interview.

Preparing Your Speech

First, logically organize it. The speech should have an introduction, a body, and a conclusion. In the introduction, clearly specify what you will be talking about. In the body, prove your case with evidence. In the conclusion, sum everything up and perhaps end with an eloquent quote or an incisive example.

Second, use a variety of evidence. Quote statistics, cite studies, employ personal examples.

Third, quote authorities. Refer to respected people (ancient and modern) who have been pro-gun (the founding fathers, ancient philosophers, economists, sociologists, civil liberties lawyers).

Fourth, practice your speech several times. If you can practice in front of others, even better.

Delivering Your Speech

First, know the time allotted for your speech. Stay within it.

Second, actually look at your audience. Keep in eye contact with them.

Third, sound natural. This means that you shouldn't simply read a prepared text. Try to memorize your speech or better yet, learn how to speak extemporaneously from notes. These notes could list your key points, your key facts, and your key rhetorical phrases.

Fourth, adapt to your audience. If you are among a small group of people, be more informal. If you are in a small room, don't bellow.

Fifth, speak loudly, clearly, firmly.

Sixth, use gestures, but vary them. Don't keep repeating the same hand movement. That's not a gesture; its a nervous habit. And its annoying. Gestures should seem to flow out from you naturally.

Seventh, particularly among smaller groups of people, avoid using a podium. Anything that comes between you and the audience helps to block communication. Of course, if you have a written speech, you will have to use a podium.

Spicing up Your Voice

When making a speech, it is extremely important to pay attention to how you sound. Is your voice flat, listless, and dull or is it full, lively and exciting? Is your voice loud and clear, or can the audience barely hear it? Speech expert Dorothy Sarnoff gives the following advice about how use your voice to best effect:

Add color to your voice with pace and pausing. You don't want to talk at a snails pace; or rattle like Morse code. Speaking about 170 words a minute is ideal. Train yourself by marking a passage in a book and timing yourself to find out if you should speed up or slow down.

Listen to your pacing. If it lacks energy, tighten your stomach muscles as if you were riding a horse and didn't want to fall off.

A nasal voice makes you sound older, negative, frustrated, hostile and cold. Letting the voice come from the chest produces a better sound.

For more information about how to make a speech, you might want to consult The Public Speakers Treasure Chest, by Herbert Prochnow (Harper and Row, New York).

Preparing for a Debate

The first thing you should do when preparing to participate in a debate about guns is to acquaint yourself with the basic arguments that you can use. This will help you come up with your opening speech and it will also show you the options you have when responding to your opponent. Listed below are the basic arguments that can be used to make the case for guns and the basic arguments that can be used to make the case against gun control. Detailed information and statistics in support of these arguments can be found in Section II of this book,

The Case for Guns

1. Guns are a Constitutional right. The Federal Constitution clearly and emphatically protects the right of the citizenry to keep and bear arms. Furthermore, many state constitutions also protect this basic right.

2. Guns are a moral right. First, the idea of liberty suggests that people ought to be able to buy and sell legitimate products without substantial government interference. Since the vast majority of guns are never used for illegal purposes, guns are

legitimate products. Therefore, we should have the liberty to buy and sell them. Second, one of the most fundamental human rights is the right to self-defense. Guns are one of the most effective means to guarantee these right. Thus, when you take guns away from people, you are depriving them of one of the most important means to effect their right of self-defense.

3. Guns may help reduce crime. Their is a substantial amount of evidence to show that high rates of gun ownership in specific areas can dramatically reduce the crime rate presumably because would-be criminals fear honest citizens who are armed.

4. A gun ban would create insufferable problems. The estimated cost of buying back guns from American citizens is $10.8 billion. And to make a gun ban truly work, the government would have to resort to gun confiscation. It would be tempted to use unconstitutional methods in order to enforce the ban. Even then the ban would most assuredly not keep guns out of the hands of the criminals only out of the hands of honest citizens.

5. Opponents of gun control span the political spectrum. There is a public perception that those who oppose gun control are kooks, crazies, or right wing nuts. The evidence suggests otherwise. A wide variety of distinguished people have come out against gun control from legislators to law professors, from conservatives to liberals. Their opposition should cause those who support gun control to take another look at the issue.

The Case Against Gun Control

1. Its unconstitutional. The Constitution guarantees individuals the right to keep and bear arms.

2. Its anti-liberty. People should have economic freedom to buy and sell legitimate products. The

vast majority of most guns are never used for illegal purposes. Therefore, the citizens economic liberty to buy and sell guns should not be infringed.

3. It wont work. Neither gun bans nor gun registration will take guns out of the hands of criminals. Studies show that most criminals don't get guns by legal methods anyway. And criminals aren't about to turn their guns in to the government.

4. Gun control will make crime worse. Criminals will become bolder when they know it is much less likely that those they victimize will have the means to fight back.

5. The cost of gun control will be prohibitive. The estimated cost for buying back peoples guns is $10.8 billion.

6. Gun control is racist. Gun control has historically been used in America to keep blacks and unpopular minorities from owning guns.

7. Gun control is sexist. Guns are one of the most effective ways women can protect themselves from being the victims of rape and assault. Making guns harder to get will punish women unfairly.

Speaking on Television

Speaking before a live audience and speaking on television are two entirely different experiences. You must come to terms with these differences if you are to be successful on TV.

Be subdued is perhaps the best advice for appearing on TV. Be subdued in your emotions; be subdued in your clothes; be subdued in the length and complexity of your answers.

Its crucial to understand that TV does not present the real you. It magnifies; it magnifies your weight (you'll look about ten pounds heavier on the air); it magnifies your emotions; it magnifies your clothes. Keeping these things in mind, here are a few TV Dos and Don'ts.

When appearing on television:

Do wear makeup. Pancake or base makeup is suggested for both men and women.

Do relax. Try to be warm and natural, not grand and imposing. Remember, you are talking to each individual viewer in his or her home. Be conversational.

Do be concise. Television is best suited for short, simple explanations using short, dramatic examples and statistics. Avoid complex answers and avoid long answers. Before going on the air, try to think up pithy phrases you can use to summarize your points.

When appearing on television:

Don't wear clothes with intricate patterns. Patterns can be convoluted by the TV camera. Avoid at all costs striped shirts, small plaids, herringbone, etc. Solids or very simple patterns are your best bets.

Don't wear bright clothes or deep colors. Avoid bright and heavily saturated colors. Muted or pastel shades are much better.

Don't wear large and shiny jewelry.

Don't wear high contrast combinations. Avoid wearing clothes that have dramatically contrasting colors things like white shirts and navy blue suits.

Don't get angry usually. It is usually the best policy to stay calm and dispassionate on TV. Your displays of emotion will only be magnified and make you look foolish. There is an exception: Sometimes calculated anger can be useful. For example, you might be discussing women who have used their guns in self-defense. In this case, you might want to show a moderate amount of anger at those gun control advocates who would leave such people without protection. "What do they expect these women to do,?!" you might say indignantly. "Turn the other cheek so that they can be battered, raped and murdered?!"

It is virtually never a good idea to get angry at the person interviewing you, however. No matter how abusive a journalist is towards you, be kind, courteous and even humorous towards him or her. If the journalist is especially stupid and arrogant, you might try condescension.

Speaking on the Radio

When being interviewed on a radio show, you have a special advantage: you can (and should) bring along a fact sheet. The fact sheet should not be a substitute for thinking on your feet; it is merely a place where you list a few choice bullets of ammunition with which to counter the opposition. Being able to cite specific studies and statistics at the drop of a hat sounds impressive remember, the audience wont be able to see you referring to the fact sheet.

Part III of this book contains a sample fact sheet that you may copy and use if you find it helpful.

Working with
Pro-Gun Groups

Grass-Roots Committees

If you choose to get involved in the political process, whether running for office or just trying to pass or defeat a particular piece of legislation, you will find that a substantial commitment of time, energy, and (usually) money is required.

You will also find that you can make a difference!

In previous chapters, I have discussed methods that are likely to achieve individual successes for you in the political arena. Writing to your Congressman, issuing statements to the local media, testifying before legislative committees all these can and do help make the difference. Unfortunately, few of us have the stamina necessary to make any definitive effect alone.

A local, grass-roots citizens committee can be one of the most successful means of maintaining your right to keep and bear arms. This kind of organization performs an important watchdog function. Through it, you are able to alert your friends, neighbors, fellow gun enthusiasts, and concerned citizens to upcoming legislation, current literature, and data of importance to the preservation of the Second Amendment. Every success you have as an individual citizen is magnified by the number of supporters you have.

Not every pro-gun rights activist is capable of maintaining the massive efforts that are needed. Not all pro-gun clubs are able to marshall the resources necessary for victory. What is the answer? One thing your local gun club might do is affiliate with a national grass-roots political action organization such as the Citizens Committee for the Right to Keep and Bear Arms. This is a good way, and sometimes the only way, to exchange information quickly and receive artillery support when you need it. Coordination is the key to political success.

These organizations are composed of concerned citizens who have joined together to protect their interests in our case, the right to keep and bear arms. Their tools are more complex than those used by the individual or local groups. They instigate investigations, gather materials for exposes, make appearances before state and federal legislative bodies, issue press releases to the national media, file lawsuits, and use other responsible tactics to accomplish your goals for you.

The information afforded you by such groups with regard to crucial legislation or supportive political candidates is essential to your success.

But such a political group cannot be successful without you. As a member, your individual efforts can be joined with thousands of other concerned citizens and achieve the greatest impact.

Involvement in the Political Process

It is not enough to become involved only with other gun enthusiasts, however. You must get out and work through the political process. In order to do this you should get involved with the party of your choice. If you are a member of a gun club, get the other members of your club involved too. Gun owners cannot afford to ignore either the Democrats or Republicans or members of third parties, for that matter. It is more important to support your principles and the men who share them than to follow a party line blindly. By working within the party structure you can reach more people and achieve greater successes. Even on the lowest levels it is possible to influence the support for the various state and local political candidates and your party's platform. On the precinct level you can propose a firearms resolution your candidate can sign. The sample that follows may be copied as is, or amended.

Sample Political Firearms Resolution

Whereas, present firearms control laws and ordinances have been unsuccessful in curtailing criminal acts involving firearms, and

Whereas, more restrictive firearms laws would only serve to infringe on the lawful acquisition of property useful in sport and defense, and

Whereas, individuals suspected of offenses involving the use of firearms have not been prosecuted to the full extent of present laws as a deterrent and/or punishment; therefore

Be It Resolved by the (name) Party of Precinct (number) to oppose further legislation restricting their acquisition, ownership, carrying, and use; to call for full and impartial enforcement of present laws and/or ordinances relation thereto; and hereby instructs its delegates to support these actions to these effects and to support candidates who will do likewise, and

Be It Further Resolved that a copy of this resolution be forwarded to the District (number) Convention of the (name) Party for consideration by the Convention for submission to the Party of consideration by the Convention for submission to the State and National Conventions of the (name) Party.

In recent elections, over 30 Congressmen and Senators who either introduced legislation favorable to the firearms owner or who voted favorably on pro-gun legislation went down to defeat. There are many reasons for this the foremost being that gun owners did not know where the candidates stood.

This year, and in future election years, our first step must be to identify our political friends and our political enemies. Kennedy, Metzenbaum, Rodino, Biaggi and the like are vocal and visible enemies. It is more difficult to discern the candidates who support the right to keep and bear arms. But that does not absolve us of the responsibility of finding out who they are so that we can support them just as fervently as we oppose our enemies.

If we band together on this issue, we have an arsenal of ammunition. Remember that there are 80 million gun owners. There have never been that many people who voted for a successful presidential candidate. If we joined together do you think any party would have an anti-gun platform? Or an anti-gun candidate? Or presidential candidate?

You can find the local offices of most major political parties listed in your yellow pages under Political Parties. If you are still unable to locate the party of your choice, contact your local Chamber of Commerce.

Section II
Gun Facts

Accidents and Guns

Everyone here has probably heard a story about someone who was killed accidentally by a gun. Perhaps you've heard about a child who found his parents' handgun and how it discharged. Or maybe you've heard a story about an adult who was carelessly handling a loaded gun and was shot to death. Such stories are surely tragic.

But they don't mean that we should get rid of guns — like the gun grabbers claim.

Living in an Unsafe World

What the gun banners fail to comprehend is that nothing is perfectly safe in this fallible world. Not driving. Not swimming. Not eating. Not owning a gun.

You'd literally have to eliminate every human activity to eliminate accidental deaths. And believe me, gun owning wouldn't be the first thing to go. Compared to other things, owning a gun is wonderfully safe. According to the Statistical Abstract of the United States, 1987 edition, there were only 1,695 firearms accidents that led to deaths in 1983 (the most recent year for which it gives figures). I say "only" quite seriously. Over 99.9% of all households with a handgun did not experience a fatal firearms accident during the year. Furthermore, accidental gun deaths account for a mere 2% of all accidental deaths in this country. [Under the Gun, pp. 15, 132]

So during 1983, for instance, when there were 1,695 deaths from firearms accidents, there were also over 44,000 deaths caused by car accidents; over 12,000 deaths caused by accidental falls; over 5,000 deaths caused by fires; and over 4,500 deaths due to accidental poisonings. That's not even mentioning the 5,254 deaths from drowning.

In other words, in 1983 you were 26 times more likely to die in a car accident than from a gun accident. You were seven times more likely to die by falling down. You were three times more likely to die by drowning and three times more likely to die by fire. You were 2.7 times more likely to die by being poisoning.

In short, if you really wanted to make the world safer, banning guns is one of the last things you'd do. First you'd ban driving, walking, swimming and eating!

The Trend in Gun Accidents

It is important to note that accidental gun deaths (and the accidental gun death rate) have been declining steadily. In 1970, there were 2,406 firearms accidents resulting in death. By 1983, that figure had fallen to 1,695. The rate of accidental gun deaths has also been decreasing. In 1970, it was 1.2 per 100,000; in 1983, it was .7 per 100,000.

[Statistical Abstract of the United States, 1987, p. 79]

Types of Gun Accidents/Accidents in the Home

Often people are most concerned about accidents in the home; thus, they are afraid to keep guns in the home because they are supposedly so unsafe. This is largely a myth. Don't get me wrong: I don't want to minimize the importance of proper care and handling of firearms; they certainly need to be treated with respect and caution. (Children, for example, shouldn't be allowed to play with them.) This being said, it is important to remember that about 40% of firearms accidents are hunting accidents. This means that the already-low accidental gun death rate is reduced even further when one considers just gun accidents in the home.

In 1985, the accidental gun death rate in the home was only .3 per 100,000 people — meaning that there was a total of 800 fatalities. While every death is tragic, and while we certainly must work to reduce the number of people killed by guns accidentally in their homes, this number of deaths is comparatively low.

For during the same year, there were 3,800 home-related poisonings; 4,000 death associated with home fires; 6,100 death from home falls; and 2,500 home suffocations. Thus, you were over four times more likely to die in a home-related poisoning than in a home gun accident; over seven times more likely to die in a home-related fall; five times more likely to die from a home fire; and over three times more likely to be suffocated. [Under the Gun, p. 15; Accident Facts 1986, National Safety Council, pp. 80-81]

B.A.T.F. Abuses

The Bureau of Alcohol, Tobacco and Firearms (BATF) is a division of the U.S. Treasury Department. In its original form, it was merely a branch of the Internal Revenue Service, and its primary responsibility was tax collection. After the passage of the Gun Control Act of 1968, however, the branch was expanded into a full bureau independent of the IRS and was handed the added responsibility of enforcing federal firearms regulations.

That's when the troubles started.

The Bureau essentially declared war on the nation's law-abiding gun owners. It began what can only be described as a reign of terror — prosecuting people for the most minor infractions of the laws, conducting warrantless searches, seizing and keeping the guns of innocent gun owners, raiding innocent people's homes.

Abuses by BATF got so bad that committees in both houses of Congress ultimately investigated the agency. So did a private task force of civil libertarians, law professors, and gun activists.

What was discovered during these investigations was nothing short of shocking. It ought to alarm anyone and everyone concerned about the state of civil liberties in our nation today.

Here are just some of the questionable Tactics that have been employed by the BATF:

Entrapment

This is where the BATF lures, tricks, or encourages a person to commit a crime so that he can then be arrested. There are several types of entrapment used by the Bureau.

First, there is entrapment against gun collectors. In this type of entrapment, a government agent will approach a gun collector or other private seller and purchase a gun. The agent may then make subsequent purchases at gun shows or other occasions, and will then arrest the seller for "dealing without a license."

What is so galling about this type of entrapment is that those arrested are often gun collectors who only sell a handful of guns a year. Why is this important? Because the BATF itself discourages these types of people from applying for licenses! Historically, the BATF has stated that those persons who sell "four to six" guns a year don't need a license. But that doesn't stop the BATF from prosecuting such persons anyway! Indeed, a former BATF agent who worked in the Montana office has testified: "It was a common joke that whenever a gun owner telephoned our office inquiring about how he could comply with BATF regulations, agents would provide false answers to the inquiries, ask who the caller was, and then set them up in entrapment situations to arrest them for the selling of firearms."

A second type of entrapment is known as the "strawman" sale. This tactic is used to arrest licensed dealers. Here a government agent or informant tries to get a licensed dealer to sell a gun to someone prohibited from buying firearms. Prohibited people include non-residents of a state, persons under age, and felons. The way this ruse works is like this: An agent or informant who is a prohibited person approaches a dealer to buy a firearm. The agent then produces out-of-state identification or indicates that he cannot sign the registration form (which contains a statement that he is not a prohibited person). The dealer invariably refuses to sell.

The "prohibited person" then suggests that someone else (usually a friend or a relative) could purchase the gun for him. If the dealer takes the bait, he will respond that he can sell to a local person provided that person can produce valid local identification and can legally fill out the purchase forms.

The prohibited person then returns with a second agent, the straw man. The straw man produces the required identification and signs the appropriate forms. The prohibited person, however, is the one who comes up with the money; at the end of the transaction the straw man steps back and the prohibited person quickly steps in to pick up the firearm. The dealer is then arrested for selling to a prohibited person.

A third type of entrapment involves machine guns, particularly those known as deactivated war trophies ("Dewats"). BATF has provided information on how legally to deactivate certain fully automatic weapons thru welding so that they may not be "readily restored" to full automatic operation. The information the Bureau provides, however, is different from the legal requirements for deactivation which it introduces at the trials of those who follow its advice!

Abusive Use of Raids

The Bureau has indiscriminately used raids without regard to the safety or the constitutional rights of those whose homes or businesses are being raided. Some of the more sordid examples include:

Silver Spring, Maryland, June 1971. Four plainclothes government agents broke down the back door of the apartment of Ken Ballew, who was in the bathtub at the time. Ballew's wife was understandably terrified and cried out to her husband. Thinking that criminals were breaking into the apartment, Ballew armed himself with a replica of a 19th century revolver. Three government agents subsequently fired upon Ballew — even though each time, Ballew did not fire back or show signs of resistance. Finally, one of the government agents succeeded in shooting Ballew in the brain. He is now permanently crippled.

San Jose, California, June 1978. About fifty armed government agents invaded the San Jose Gun and Antique Show. With them came fire engines, a SWAT team, and a large group of reporters who had apparently been briefed and invited along. For about two hours, the agents blocked the exits and refused to permit persons inside the building to leave. In the meantime, some agents photographed the occupants while others announced, thru the P.A. system, that all participants would be obligated to identify themselves and to sign Treasury documents which would be provided.

And what was the reason for the employment of these Gestapo-like tactics? What were those at the Gun and Antique Show doing that they deserve to be subjected to such police-state measures? Perhaps the participants were neo-Nazis planning to overthrow the government? Not quite. Why then, this wholesale disregard for civil liberties? Well, reportedly the BATF had heard claims that some participants of the show were selling guns without local licenses or without fulfilling the required paperwork. So the BATF decided to distribute pamphlets to the show's participants that explained the laws applicable to firearms sales. And it further decided to use draconian methods to do so. It was somewhat like trying to kill a fly with a sledge-hammer. And yet, characteristically, the BATF thought it had done nothing wrong!

Kirkland, Washington, October 1978. In a paramilitary style operation, government agents invaded the neighborhood of Mr. and Mrs. Elmer Turngren. A four-block area was sealed off, the neighborhood evacuated, and the Turngren home surrounded. Some of the agents ransacked their home, while others stood over the family with automatic rifles. At the time of the raid, Mr. Turngren had been asleep and his wife was reading a Bible lesson. The only other person living there was their grade-school-aged daughter.

Seizures of Property

Every year the Bureau confiscates thousands of firearms. The way in which these confiscations are made raises serious questions about the ultimate fairness of BATF actions.

First, the Bureau seems to confiscate a disproportionate number of relatively harmless guns. That is, instead of confiscating those types of guns used in crimes, the Bureau seems intent on confiscating private collections of antique and long arm guns. A study conducted using records gained through the Freedom of Information Act showed that only 40% of confiscated arms were handguns. And only 4.04% were "Saturday Night Specials" by the Bureau's own definition!

Furthermore, the Bureau is extremely reluctant to return the guns once they have been confiscated — even when the gun owners have been acquitted from any wrong-doing in a criminal court of law. Indeed, if a gun owner is acquitted in a criminal trial, the Bureau then often attempts to try him on the exact same charge in a civil trial — keeping his guns in the meantime. Such was the case with Patrick Mulcahey. Mr. Mulcahey was arrested for dealing in firearms without a license. He was acquitted by a jury of all wrong-doing. But that didn't mean he got his guns back. Instead, BATF filed a civil suit against him on the same charges. As Mr. Mulcahey awaited his second trial, the Bureau still held on to his guns — some two years after his acquittal.

Or take another example: Bureau agents seized the collection of Gus Cargyle based upon allegations that he had engaged in dealing without a license and possessed an illegal machine gun. Three months later, charges still had not been filed. Cargyle sued to force the return of his firearms. During a hearing for that suit it was discovered why no charges had been filed: First, the supposedly illegal machine gun was in fact welded up and inoperable. And the dealership allegations fell through when it turned out that Cargyle had not sold a single firearm to Bureau agents. The only support for the charge was the statement of a person who was then hospitalized and under sedation. Needless to say, Cargyle's suit was successful. The court ordered the return of his firearms.

But still, the Bureau refused! Only after the BATF was taken before a court again did it finally return the arms! Upon their return, it was discovered that they had been stored in a damp warehouse and permitted to rust!

This helps to point out yet another flagrant abuse of gun confiscations by the BATF — namely, the deliberate damage inflicted on the firearms seized. Here are some examples: A Colorado man had his gun collection seized after a gun show. While he was being booked in at a federal office, his collection was inventoried in the same room. The agents reportedly removed each firearm from its padded carrying case, recorded its description and then (without replacing it back in its case), pitched it across the room to a corner where the firearms were permitted to pile up. Among the firearms so treated was the collector's pride, a Parker shotgun valued at $10,000. In the words of the collector's attorney, "it nearly killed him."

Another example: A Virginia dealer reported that his firearms were stacked in piles on the floor and brought to trial piled into a 50-gallon drum. The agents pulling the firearms from the drum in the courtroom appeared excessively rough, so he requested that they take greater care. They responded by slamming them down, one atop another, on the tables in the room. The dealer's attorney confirmed this occurrence.

Another dealer in Arizona reported an even more callous approach. Taken from him were firearms, held under federal license, which were of great value to military collectors. Their value was greatly increased by their being in the original military issue boxes, sealed with the original metal bands. The agents were obviously preparing to open the boxes, and the collector pointed out that this would reduce their value. He suggested that since the original seals were in place and the outside of the boxes listed the firearms and serial number, they had but to copy the same. The agents responded by dragging two of the boxed firearms outside, and then using a sledge to bash open the boxes.

One might have thought that after such abuses were revealed, the BATF would be shamed into stopping them. But there is some evidence that this has not happened.

In 1985, the BATF seized nearly 40 guns in a raid on the home of Scott LeNoble in Florida. Thirty-five of the firearms were later returned, but LeNoble says that BATF agents damaged the firearms before returning them. His neighbors back him up on this. And he has videotapes of the officers "throwing the guns down on the ground."

Two years after the raid, in 1987, the BATF has still refused to return a .30 caliber M-1 carbine and a .22 magnum, two shot derringer in a wallet holster. The BATF charges that these firearms were not registered.

But LeNoble insists that neither gun needs to be registered. The M-1, he says is completely unusable — it's not only torch-cut through the right siderail, but the barrel is an unchambered factory reject that won't accept "any known round — period...." The second gun, meanwhile, has in the past been excluded from registration by the BATF itself! According to LeNoble, the BATF sent out notices to gun dealers indicating that derringers in wallet holsters don't have to be registered.

The two guns are only worth from $100 - $250, but for LeNoble this is a matter of principle. And so he has spent some $15,000 on legal fees so far just to fight the BATF. As an honest citizen, he feels his rights have been trampled on:

"I've played by the rules my entire life," he explained to Gun Week. "I'm a Nam vet. I've got a wife and three kids. I was working two jobs (before he lost them because of the BATF bust), doing the whole nine yards — and I collected guns. And for that I've been persecuted — not prosecuted, persecuted."

[For more information, see Gun Week, April 3, 1987, The Rights of Gun Owners (pp. 30-55) and The BATF's War on Civil Liberties]

The Constitution

The right to keep and bear arms is a fundamental liberty guaranteed by the Second Amendment to the United States Constitution. The Second Amendment is elegant, explicit, emphatic: "A well-regulated militia, being necessary to the security of a free state, the right of the people to keep and bear arms shall not be infringed." What could possibly be clearer than this?

Unfortunately, to many people today the meaning of this amendment isn't clear. Perhaps this has something to do with the persistent misinformation spread about by gun control advocates. Anti-gunners like to argue that because the Second Amendment talks about "a well-regulated militia" its provisions apply only to the state governments. In other words, the states have the right to arm a military force (like the National Guard) without interference from the federal government.

But this interpretation is, quite simply, ridiculous. It would make the Founding Fathers roll over in their graves. It has no basis in either constitutional history or in American jurisprudence.

What the Founders Meant by "Militia"

The authors of the Constitution were emphatic about what they meant by the Second Amendment. They saw it as a guarantee to every able-bodied man to keep a gun in his home and bear it outside the home. Indeed, the use of the word "militia" helps to prove this point, not cast doubt on it. For at the time the Constitution was written, the word "militia" did not refer to a select group of individuals like the National Guard. It referred to every able-bodied man in each state. Even under current law, this is still the case. The U.S. Code, Title 10, section 31 states that the militia of each state includes "all able-bodied males at least 17 years of age and… under 45 years of age who are, or have made declaration of intention to become, citizens." And it's interesting to note that up until the early years of the 20th century, almost every free adult male was actually required by federal law to own a firearm and a minimum supply of ammunition and military equipment! The right to keep and bear arms, then, is an individual right, not a collective one. Each law-abiding person has the right to arm himself individually.

The Cultural Context of the Second Amendment

In order to truly appreciate the significance of the Second Amendment, it might be a good idea to briefly review the cultural context in which the Amendment was written. The right to keep and bear arms didn't just begin with the Constitution, after all; it had a long, distinguished history — both here in America and across the ocean in England.

Blackstone in his famous Commentaries on the Laws of England, for example, included the right to arms as one of the five "absolute rights" of an Englishman. The Founding Fathers felt the same way — as can be aptly demonstrated from numerous quotes. Richard Henry Lee, a signer of the Declaration of Independence, declared: "To preserve liberty, it is essential that the whole body of the people always possess arms, and be taught alike, especially when young, how to use them."

Lee's quote points out why the Founding Fathers considered the right of arms so crucial. They viewed it as a guard against tyranny; a check against the usurping of the people's rights. They argued that government could not easily impose a dictatorship upon a populace that had the means to resist. Alternately, they thought that forbidding arms to the general public was one way to ensure the success of tyranny. As Constitutional Convention delegate George Mason put it: "[T]o disarm the people... was the best and most effectual way to enslave them." Or as Noah Webster said: "Before a standing army can rule, the people must be disarmed."

Other Reasons the Founding Fathers Supported Guns

There were other reasons that the Founding Fathers supported the right to bear arms, of course. Some of these were mentioned in a group of proposals submitted to the Constitutional Convention by Pennsylvania delegates. Their proposals declared that "the people have a right to bear arms for the defense of themselves and their own state, or the United States, or for the purpose of killing game...." In 1788, John Adams similarly argued that "arms in the hands of citizens may be used at individual discretion" for the defense of the country, the overthrow of tyranny or "private self-defense."

Current Interpretation of the Second Amendment

There have been only three Supreme Court rulings on the Second Amendment. The most recent — and the only one to give an extended analysis to the Amendment — was handed down in 1939. The case was United States v. Miller. In that case, the Court ruled that a ban on the interstate transport of sawed-off shotguns was not on its face unconstitutional. The gist of this ruling is that while the Second Amendment does apply to individuals, it doesn't necessarily guarantee the right to hold all weapons — only those somehow related to the maintenance of the militia.

It is important to note that Miller filed no brief — and made no argument — before the Supreme Court. Only the prosecution presented a case.

Second Amendment scholar Donald Kates explains: "[Miller] steers an almost perfect middle course between today's contending extremes — those who claim that the amendment guarantees nothing to individuals versus those who claim that its guarantee is unlimited. Far from upholding the state's rights position, the Court clearly recognized that the defendants could claim the amendment's protection as individuals, and that, in doing so, they need not prove themselves members of some formal military unit like the National Guard. At the same time the Court's focus on the weapon suggests rational limitations on the kinds of arms that the amendment guarantees to individuals. Such arms must be both of the kind in 'common use' at the present time and probably 'part of ordinary military equipment.' "

[Kates, "Handgun Prohibition, " pp. 221-223, 250-251; also The Rights of Gun Owners, pp. 4-14]

Critics of Gun Control

Advocates of gun control love to caricature those who are skeptical of gun control as unthinking, uncaring "right-wing gun nuts."

Nothing could be further from the real truth. The opponents of gun control span the political spectrum. Many aren't even gun owners. Many are respected lawyers, professors, and legislators. These distinguished and vocal critics of anti-gun schemes have included:

The late Senator Frank Church (D-ID), one of the most outspoken liberals to have been elected to the United States Senate.

Roy Innis, national chairman of the Congress on Racial Equality.

Lawyer Mark K. Benenson, former American chairman for Amnesty International.

Judge Kenneth Chotiner, former vice president of the ACLU of Southern California.

David T. Hardy, an attorney who specializes in consumer fraud and civil rights litigation.

Don B. Kates, Jr., an attorney who drafted civil rights legislation for the House Judiciary Committee and held administrative positions with California Rural Legal Assistance.

Particularly noteworthy for mention are the following two people. These scholars originally supported gun control. Then they began to study the issue. They conducted a comprehensive review of the literature on weapons, crime and violence in the United States using a grant from the National Institute of Justice. During this study, they came to the common sense conclusion that eliminating guns won't eliminate violent crime. The scholars are:

James Wright, professor of sociology at the University of Massachusetts, Amherst and director of the Social and Demographic Research Institute. He is the author of six books.

Peter Rossi, professor of sociology at the University of Massachusetts, Amherst, director of research at the Social and Demographic Research Institute, and past president of the American Sociological Association. Widely regarded as one of the most eminent American social scientists, Dr. Rossi has authored 20 books.

[Restricting Handguns, Under the Gun, The BATF's War on Civil Liberties, *Gun Week* (August 8, 1986), p. 12]

Foreign Countries

The fundamental argument made by gun control advocates is actually quite simple: Gun ownership causes crime. America has a lot of guns, therefore America has a lot of crime. Eliminate the guns, and you will eliminate the crime.

On its face, this argument is rather silly. Then how do gun control advocates justify it? Good question.

One of the key ways is by resorting to foreign examples. Gun control advocates relish pointing out that European countries with strict gun control laws have lower violent crime rates than the United States. They immediately infer from this that the difference in crime rates is due to a difference in the number of guns owned.

But this is ludicrous.

The record clearly demonstrates that gun control laws have nothing to do with the difference in crime rates between Europe and America.

The British Example

Take Britain, for instance. Gun control supporters love to use this example. They say "Look! Britain has tough gun control laws. And its murder rate is lower than America's." So? It's certainly not because of gun control! In the 1920s, before Britain had its restrictive gun laws, the British murder rate was still less than

America's. Obviously, then, the difference in homicide rates is due to something more than just gun control.

And if one compares the murder rates in Britain and America since the time Britain passed its gun laws, one makes a startling discovery: The British homicide rate has been increasing in a much more dramatic fashion than the U.S. rate! From 1930 - 1975 the U.S. rate went up 30% From 1960 - 1975, the British homicide rate doubled!

So if anything, the British gun control laws have helped to spur murders, not hindered them!

Other Examples that Disprove Gun-Crime "Link"

But let's not stop with Britain. Gun control advocates' rhetoric to the contrary, the international record clearly demonstrates a dearth of evidence supporting a positive link between guns and crime rates.

Indeed, the four nations with the highest per capita gun ownership also have some of the world's lowest crime rates. I'm talking about those countries gun controllers rarely talk about because they don't fit their preconceived ideas — Switzerland, Israel, Denmark, and Finland.

International Evidences for a Gun Control - Crime Link

But let's not stop with just showing that there's no positive link between guns and crime. The experience in some nations suggests that low gun ownership rates might be linked to higher crime rates. Consider these examples:

- Taiwan: Taiwan imposes a virtual ban on handguns. Yet its homicide rate is twice the U.S. average.

- Mexico: Mexico has a low gun ownership rate. Yet it has a much higher crime rate than ours.

- Jamaica: In 1974, Jamaica outlawed the private ownership of all firearms and ammunition.

Possession of a single bullet was punishable by life in prison. Yet six years after the imposition of this Draconian gun prohibition, Jamaica had six times as many gun deaths per capita as Washington, D.C. — one of the most violent cities in America.

[Seven Myths of Gun Control]

Our Founding Fathers

If our Founding Fathers were alive today, they would no doubt be members of a pro-gun group. That statement might sound rather wild; but really, if one knows Colonial history, it's not. Indeed, it is hard to overstate how much our Founding Fathers cherished the firearm. Their writings are replete with references extolling its virtues.

Bulwark Against Tyranny

The chief virtue they noted, of course, was political. They saw arms as a bulwark against tyranny. An armed populace was much more likely to be a free populace. Oppositely, a disarmed populace was virtually writing an invitation for tyranny. These truths were repeated time after time in many different ways. Here are just a few examples:

"Before a standing army can rule, the people must be disarmed; as they are in almost every kingdom in Europe. The supreme power in America cannot enforce unjust laws by the sword, because the whole body of the people are armed, and constitute a force superior to any band of regular troops that can be, on any pretense, raised in the United States." — Noah Webster, An Examination into the Leading Principles of the Federal Constitution (1787).

"To preserve liberty, it is essential that the whole body of the people always possess arms and be taught alike, especially when young, how to use them." — Richard Lee, Letters from the Federal Farmer, 169-170.

"Guard with jealous attention the public liberty. Suspect everyone who approaches that jewel. Unfortunately, nothing will preserve it but downright force. Whenever you give up that force you are ruined... The great object is that every man be armed... Everyone who is able may have a gun." — Patrick Henry.

"As civil rulers, not having their duty to the people duly before them, may attempt to tyrannize, and as the military forces which must be occasionally raised to defend our country, might pervert their power to the injury of their fellow citizens, the people are confirmed in their right to keep and bear their private arms." — Tench Coxe, "Remarks on the First Part of the Amendments to the Federal Constitution," Philadelphia Federal Gazette, June 23, 1789.

"A government resting on a minority is an aristocracy, not a Republic, and could not be safe with a numerical and physical force against it, without a standing army, an enslaved press, and a disarmed populace." (emphasis added) — James Madison, The Federalist Papers (No. 46).

Americans need never fear their government because of "the advantage of being armed, which the Americans possess over the people of almost every other nation." — James Madison, The Federalist Papers (No. 46).

Guns Virtuous in General

Of course, the Founding Fathers didn't like guns solely as a defense against political tyranny. This can

be shown from the following quote from Thomas
Jefferson:

"A strong body makes the mind strong. As to the
species of exercises, I advise the gun. While this gives
a moderate exercise to the Body, it gives boldness,
enterprise and independence to the mind. Games played
with the ball, and others of that nature, are too violent
for the body and stamp no character on the mind. Let
your gun therefore be the constant companion of your
walks."

[That Every Man Be Armed, and The Rights of Gun
Owners.]

Gun Control

The cardinal problem with gun control is simple, really: It won't work. Neither gun bans nor gun registration will take guns out of the hands of criminals. Even if they did, the criminals would use other weapons to inflict their wounds. If we really want to attack the roots of crime, we must attack the criminals — not the instruments that they pervert for their own twisted ends.

Unfortunately, those who advocate gun control can't see these simple truths — so they keep pushing the same tired proposals.

Here are some quick critiques of different forms of gun control:

Gun Bans

Gun bans won't work. First off, effective enforcement would be impossible. "If we take the highest plausible value for the total number of gun incidents in any given year — 1,000,000 — and the lowest plausible value for the total number of firearms now in private hands — 100,000,000 — we see rather quickly that the guns now owned exceed the annual incident count by a factor of at least 100. This means that the existing stock is adequate to supply all conceivable criminal purposes for at least the next century, even if the worldwide manufacture of new guns were halted today and if each presently owned firearm were used criminally once and only once. Short of an outright house-to-house search and seizure mission, just how are we going to achieve some significant reduction in the number of firearms available?" [Sociologists James Wright, Peter Rossi and Kathleen Daly, in Under the Gun, p. 320]

Some might indeed suggest house-to-house searches. But indiscriminate searches without evidence of wrongdoing are clearly unconstitutional. Even if we did conduct such a confiscation program, however, the odds would be against us. "We would have to confiscate at least 100 guns to get just one that, in any given year, would have otherwise been involved in some sort of unfortunate firearms incident." [Under the Gun, p. 320]

Even if all current guns could be successfully confiscated, that wouldn't keep guns out of the hands of criminals. A black market would spring up and flourish — just like during Prohibition. As sociologists Wright, Rossi and Daly point out: "It is, after all, not much more difficult to manufacture serviceable firearms in one's basement than to brew up a batch of home-made gin. Afghanistani tribesmen, using wood fires and metal-working equipment that is much inferior to what can be ordered through a Sears catalog, hand-craft rifles that fire the Russian AK-47 cartridge. Do we anticipate a lesser ability from American do-it-yourselfers or the Mafia?" [Under the Gun, p. 321]

Aside from the question of workability, we must also think about cost. You simply can't deprive people of their lawful property without compensation. If existing handguns are banned, then they ought to be bought back. The cost of buying back all handguns in America, however, has been estimated at an astronomical $10.8 billion. If we had a ban on all guns — both handguns and long guns, that cost would include an additional $21.6 billion to $43.2 billion! [Rights of Gun Owners, p. 17] Are Americans willing to pay this much for something that won't even work? No! Indeed, public opinion polls show that the majority of Americans oppose both handgun bans and gun confiscation. Even an anti-gun poll sponsored by the Center for the Study and Prevention of Handgun Violence demonstrates this. According to that 1978 poll, some 58% of Americans oppose a ban on the future manufacture and sale of all handguns. Further, some 62% of Americans oppose using public funds to buy back and destroy existing handguns on a mandatory basis. [Under the Gun, Table 11-2, p. 224]

Saturday Night Special Bans

A more limited gun control proposal, though just as deadly, is that of a ban on "Saturday Night Specials." "Saturday Night Specials" have no universal definition — but are generally thought of as those handguns which are cheap and small (making them easily concealable). It is commonly suggested that such guns are more likely to be used in crimes than other guns. However, the evidence here is contradictory. In general, when considering the caliber of a gun, its barrel length, and its monetary value, studies show that "Saturday Night Specials" comprise only from 25 - 33% of confiscation samples. [Under the Gun, pp. 188] So legislation attacking these guns (even if they could be defined precisely) wouldn't affect the vast majority of guns used in crime.

But this is the least of the problems with "Saturday Night Special" bans. Perhaps the most serious defect with such proposals is that they would actually increase crime fatalities caused by guns.

With other guns on the market, criminals surely wouldn't stop buying firearms just because "Saturday Night Specials" were banned. Instead, they'd buy more expensive and more deadly guns. If one's definition of a "Saturday Night Special" specifies those of a lower caliber, then criminals would be encouraged to shift from low caliber guns to a wide variety of larger caliber handguns. The larger caliber handguns. The larger caliber handguns are inherently more accurate. If fired, they are much more likely to kill someone. Thus, there could well be more fatalities.

There is at least one more glaring problem with a ban on Saturday Night Specials. This one is explained by Ernest Van den Haag. He reasons that both the poor and the elderly are the chief victims of crime and cannot necessarily afford expensive handguns for self-defense. Therefore, if you ban Saturday Night Specials, you may be taking away from them one of their only means for self-protection.

Handgun Bans

A general handgun ban would involve all of the problems previously mentioned. It would also promote a substitution effect even worse than that of an inexpensive "Saturday Night Special" ban.

For if handguns really could be effectively banned, criminals would turn to other weapons. Even if only 30% of the criminals chose long guns as substitutes (and the remaining 70% took knives) — even in this scenario, there would still be a substantial net increase in homicides according to one study! This is because long guns are inherently more accurate and devastating than handguns. They are much more likely to kill someone. ["Firearms and Firearms Regulation," pp. 272-274]

Gun Registration

Gun registration is not needed. It doesn't do anything useful. It doesn't help trace guns to criminals for the simple reason that criminals don't register their guns. In fact, the United States Supreme Court even ruled in 1968 that criminals couldn't be compelled to register their weapons because to do so would infringe on their Fifth Amendment right against self-incrimination! [Rights of Gun Owners, p. 19]

The danger with gun registration is that it might be the prelude to gun confiscation. It has happened in the past. The Nazis used Danish gun registration lists to take guns away from the Danes. [Gun Control, Kukla, p.

440] Military leaders in Greece, meanwhile, conducted a massive gun confiscation effort that wouldn't have been possible without the prior registration of firearms. [Myths About Guns, p. 50]

Waiting Periods

Another popular gun control proposal at this time is for there to be a waiting period before you can actually get the gun you want to purchase. In other words, you would apply for the gun and then wait — maybe 72 hours, maybe six months!

The claim is that during this time the police can check a gun purchaser's background, to insure that he is legally entitled to buy a gun. Gun control supporters claim that the intent of such a waiting period is to keep guns out of criminals' hands.

The effect of such "waiting periods," however is to keep guns out of everyone's hands. Often waiting periods are weeks long. Such long waiting periods make it virtually impossible for law-abiding citizens to get a gun when they need it. This is most obvious in the case of self-protection. For instance, suppose there have been a rash of armed, night-time robberies in your neighborhood. You're worried. So you want a gun. But what happens if you must wait half-a-month to actually get that gun? Or even half-a-week? By then, it may be too late.

Of course, if this proposal really would keep guns out of the hands of criminals, a short waiting period (say 48 hours) might be worth it.

But waiting periods won't work!

It is important to remember that most criminals do not get guns from legal sources to begin with. A 1985 Justice Department study showed that only 21 percent of felons' handguns were obtained through retail channels. If detailed background checks were put in place, there would not even be that many who would legally purchase guns. Thus, this proposal would not stop criminals from getting guns.

Gun control supporters like to cite anecdotes to try to prove otherwise. One of the examples that they love to use is the case of John Hinckley, who attempted to assassinate President Reagan in 1981. Sarah Brady, the wife of Presidential Press Secretary James Brady who was also shot by Hinckley, implies that had there been a mandatory waiting period for a background check, Hinckley wouldn't have gotten his gun. This is a patent falsehood. In fact, Hinckley's purchase of the gun was completely legal — and would have been completely legal under a waiting period law! Congressman Bob Stump explains: "[T]he Secret Service found that Hinckley purchased his weapon in Texas six months before shooting the President. As required, he showed proof of his Texas residency, had no felony record and had not been adjudicated mentally ill."

Gun control supporters have falsely claimed that a background check of Hinckley would have discovered that he did not live at the Texas address he listed. But this argument is specious. James Baker, from the NRA's Institute for Legislative Action, explained in testimony before Congress:

"[Hinckley] was using a valid Texas driver's license issued May 23, 1979, to make his firearms purchases. The contention that a background check would have 'uncovered' the fact that he did not physically reside at the address listed on his license is a willful distortion of the criminal record check made by local police. To the contrary, had a check been run and all criminal records been thorough and completely available, they would have confirmed that Hinckley was not a prohibited person and that his last known address was in Lubbock, Texas."

Perhaps the most serious drawback of the waiting period proposal is that any conceivable benefits would be more than outweighed by the enormous costs. If the police really wanted to catch the few criminals who do purchase guns from legal sources, they literally would have to spend millions of dollars and thousands of man-hours investigating the backgrounds of gun purchasers.

Congressman Bob Stump believes that this time and money "would be better spent investigating, prosecuting and punishing those responsible for 80 percent of our crime problem — the career criminals."

I agree.

Permit Systems

Many communities and states have established permit laws governing gun ownership. Ostensibly, permit laws are better than outright gun bans. In theory, at least, they provide a legal way for law-abiding citizens to carry firearms on their person. In practice, however, permit systems offer the worst of both possible worlds. They offer the illusion of liberty while denying its substance. In those communities where permit systems have been put into place, they often are carried out in a discriminatory, arbitrary and capricious manner.

There are basically two types of permits: premises permits and carrying permits.

Premises permits are required to have a gun in your home. Carry permits are required for you to carry guns on your person in public. Perhaps one of the most notorious premises permit systems in existence is in New York. Writes lawyer Don Kates:

"New York decided in 1957... that target shooting was no longer a legitimate reason for handgun ownership; permits would henceforth be issued only to businessmen, security guards, and a select few wanting guns for their own protection. By the early 1970s, this policy of progressively limiting permits given to ordinary citizens had reduced premises permits to less than one-seventh the number issued in London (although New York City was estimated to have one to two million unpermitted handguns). When New York appellate courts held that applicants could only be rejected if found unfit, New York City simply ignored the rulings. When the gun lobby obtained injunctions forcing the city to comply, it did, but only after establishing a two-year wait to obtain the gun-permit form. Finally, when the New York legislature reaffirmed the court decision and ordered that permit approvals or denials be made within six months, the city imposed an enormous processing fee, making application and renewal economically feasible only for the well-to-do." [The Battle Over Gun Control, p. 3]

Carry permit laws are more prevalent — and more deadly to the honest citizen who wants to defend himself or herself. Most violent crimes happen outside the home, so to walk the streets without any effective defense can be an invitation for mugging, rape and murder. Anti-gun groups sometimes claim that under carry permit systems, anyone who "truly needs" to carry a gun can get a permit. They claim that the laws only weed out those for whom it would be illegal to own guns — liked convicted felons.

They're lying.

Virtually every place that carry permit laws are in place, it is either impossible or impractical for ordinary citizens to get gun permits. A rundown of some of the worst offenders:

- New York City, New York: Admittedly, if you are rich, wealthy and famous, you can probably get a gun carry permit in New York City. If you're an ordinary citizen, however, don't even try. Ordinary law-abiding citizens are routinely denied permits, even if they have been mugged before. One noteworthy refusenik: Bernhard Goetz. On the other side of the fence, the rich and famous that have managed to get carry permits despite the restrictions include: David, John, Laurence, and Winthrop Rockefeller, Leland DuPont, Robert Goulet, Sid Caesar, Donald Trump, William

Buckley, Michael Korda, Arthur Godfrey, and Lyman Bloomingdale.

- San Fransisco, California: In 1980, only one carry permit was issued in the entire city. It went to then-Supervisor (now Mayor) Diane Feinstein, after her house was machine-gunned by the New World Liberation Front. Those ordinary folk who lived in crime-infested San Fransisco neighborhoods and wanted carry permits so they could deal with knife and gun-wielding thugs had no such luck.

- Denver, Colorado: Due to an anti-gun onslaught by Police Chief Tom Coogan and others, the number carry permits in Denver have been slashed 85% since 1983 — from 500 to 75. Under Coogan, a review board was set up to scrutinize every application and recommend to the chief whether or not to issue a permit. Applicants must undergo intensive and time consuming background checks and pass a tough test at a police firing range as well as a written examination on gun safety.

- But that's not all. The Denver City Council also hiked permit fees from $75 to $100 and annual renewal fees from $25 to $35.

- Finally, Denver District Judge Robert Kingsley forced the list of permit holders to be made public, and the Rocky Mountain News subsequently published the names. Existing permit holders have thus been stripped of their rights to privacy and the door has been opened to possible public ridicule. (Hypocritically, Judge Kingsley excluded judges and other "high ranking law enforcement officers" from his disclosure order, saying that it was no one's business which judges were armed!)

- Not surprisingly, only 33 people granted permits by former Police Chief Art Dill in 1983 are still permitted to be armed.

What is perhaps most amazing in all of this is the cowardly double-standard adopted by some outspoken gun control proponents. In public, these people rant and rave about allowing people to own guns; in private, it turns out, many of them own guns! The one positive result of the public disclosure of gun permit lists is that it has unmasked this blatant hypocrisy on the part of the gun bashers. According to the records, prominent gun control advocates with gun permits have included: John Lindsay, the late Nelson Rockefeller, Arthur Sulzberger (publisher of the New York Times), San Fransisco Mayor Diane Feinstein, and the husband of Joyce Brothers. (Joyce Brothers, it is interesting to note, claims that gun ownership indicates male sexual dysfunction.)

Such duplicity is morally reprehensible and completely indefensible; these people grab for themselves the very protection they would deny others. The bottom line is that they are afraid to practice what they preach! In this one thing, I agree with them: They have good reason to be afraid.

Mandatory Sentences

Most pro-gun groups and their supporters favor mandatory sentences for criminals who use a gun in a crime.

Anti-gun groups have tried to capitalize on the support for such measures by peddling a similar-sounding proposal that in actuality would condemn the honest as well as the guilty.

What the anti-gun groups advocate are mandatory sentences not for criminals who use guns, but for anyone who is found carrying an unlicensed gun.

The difference is enormous.

Such mandatory sentencing laws as advocated by the National Coalition to Ban Handguns aren't simply unfair; they are barbaric. Imagine what it would mean: Everyone who uses an unlicensed gun for self-defense will face a mandatory prison term because the law does not differentiate between criminal and victim. When one recalls that in many cities it is virtually impossible for ordinary citizens to get carry permits, one realizes that virtually every person who uses a gun for self-defense will be subject to a mandatory sentence.

No, you might say, this could never happen. Not in America. The people wouldn't stand for it.

But it already has happened.

In Massachusetts, for example, a man was recently prosecuted for carrying a handgun with which he had defended himself against a knife attack by a convicted felon. The man was (in the words of the state supreme court) "a hardworking family man, without a criminal record, who was respected by his fellow employees." The state's high court intimated that it wanted to let him go. But the mandatory sentencing law stripped the court of any power to do so. The man went to prison.

Effect on Crime

The underlying argument for virtually all gun control measures is that they will somehow reduce crime. In fact, the opposite is true. Gun control measures will ultimately make crime worse because they only take guns away from honest citizens, not criminals. Criminals will simply become bolder when they know it is much less likely that those they victimize will have guns.

This seems to be confirmed by surveys of prison inmates. Reports criminology professor Gary Kleck and sociologist David Bordua: "There is some direct evidence that criminals do take victim gun ownership into consideration in planning crimes and choosing victims. Convicted robbers and burglars interviewed in a California state prison stated that they would take into consideration the presence of weapons in a house or business and that they knew of specific cases where robberies were not committed because the prospective victim was known to be armed... Furthermore, the available evidence indicates that criminals perceive gun control measures as facilitating their criminal activities. In an informal survey, Menard (Illinois) Correctional Center convicts in prison for armed robbery unanimously agreed that a recent Morton Grove, Illinois ordinance banning handgun ownership would be useless in curbing crime and would make things a bit easier for them... Another such survey (by a convicted armed robber) of 100 convicts in an Ohio prison indicated that the majority of inmates thought that crimes would increase if civilian guns were confiscated, especially daylight robbery of businesses and homes." ["Firearms and Firearms Regulation," p. 283]

Media Bias

Certainly one of the most troubling aspects of the whole gun control issue is the way in which the media covers it. To be blunt, media discussion of the gun issue is often one-sided, irrelevant, and fallacious.

Evidence of Bias

According to one study, for example, anti-gun messages get 37 inches of print for every inch given to pro-gun messages. Of course, in the electronic media, the situation is somewhat better: There the gap is only seven to one! That is, anti-gun messages get 7 minutes of airtime for every one-minute given to pro-gun messages.

Another study, this time of national magazines, came up with similar results. This study was exhaustive. It covered fifteen major national magazines — including *Time*, *Newsweek*, *Harper's*, *The Atlantic Monthly* and *Reader's Digest*. It studied every article published on the gun control issue in these magazines over a ten year period — from 1968 to 1978. The conclusion? Let me quote the study's author, Dr. Gary Bullert, then professor of political science at Seattle University: "National magazine coverage of the gun control issue over the past ten years has been invariably prejudiced against the right to keep and bear arms... the major magazines in America seem totally oblivious to the rational, empirical, and scholarly pro-gun case." (emphasis added)

To be fair, since this magazine study was done in 1978, there have appeared pro-gun or reasonably balanced articles in publications like *Harper's*, *Commonweal*, and *Esquire*. But these are still far and few between; they seem to reflect little more than tokenism on the part of magazine publishers.

Why this Bias Isn't Surprising

Perhaps this evidence of bias shouldn't be surprising. After all, many media people are actually members of the gun-control movement. Although no scientific study has been undertaken about anti-gunners in the media, there's no denying that many key media people are anti-gun. Just consider how many contributed financially to the campaign for Proposition 15 in California in 1982. What was Proposition 15? It was an initiative that had it passed would have banned the sale of all new handguns. How anti-gun can you get! Here's the roster of media people who donated to the cause: Mary McGrory, columnist with the *Washington Post*; the late Frank Reynolds, ABC World News Tonight anchor; W.E. Chilton III, publisher of the Charleston Gazette; J. Cahill Pfeiffer, former chairman of NBC; Frank Stanton, former president of CBS; Richard Reeves, syndicated columnist; Edward Thompson, editor-in-chief of *Reader's Digest*.

The Types of Bias

There are at least two different ways that the media bias their coverage of the gun issue: ignoring and distorting.

Ignoring

By ignoring events and studies that support pro-gun arguments, the media can deprive the public of the data needed in order to make an informed judgement about the issue. There are no doubt many people who would like to be pro-gun — but feel awkward about it.

Why? Because they think that the only people who support guns are somehow zealots, nuts, or crazies. They aren't told about the first-rate legal minds and intellectuals who support the right to keep and bear arms; they aren't told about the respected police chiefs who support gun freedoms. They aren't told about those researchers who have cooly and dispassionately looked at the evidence and decided that gun control simply won't work. Nor do they hear about the civil libertarians who are concerned about the threats to civil liberties that gun control measures cause.

Consider some examples:

Wright and Rossi study. In 1981, social scientists James Wright and Peter Rossi published a landmark study called Weapons, Crime and Violence in America. It was an exhaustive critical review of the studies on the link between weapons and crime and violence. Its conclusion? "The prospects for ameliorating the problem of criminal violence through stricter controls over civilian ownership, purchase, or use of firearms are dim." In other words, gun control won't work.

What was so astounding about this study was the fact that its authors had originally started out in favor of gun control! It was only after examining the evidence that they made an unprecedented shift. Two years after the study was published, they came out with a book for the public.

The major media couldn't have cared less. With few exceptions, the book was ignored.

This is despite the fact that review copies were sent to all of the magazines and major newspapers that regularly review books. This is despite the fact that Wright and Rossi were not some hired hacks. They were scientists with stellar reputations. Rossi, in fact, is a past president of the American Sociological Association, with 200 books and over 125 articles and papers to his credit.

The experience with the Wright and Rossi book is not an isolated example; it is not the only scholarly pro-gun book to be spiked by the media. In 1978, the Bullert study of national magazines stated: "Sophisticated [pro-gun] books like Robert Kukla's Gun Control or James Whisker's Our Vanishing Freedom were not even reviewed, much less cited."

Distorting

The major media are also quite adept at distorting the gun issue. The way they report events related to gun control and the use of firearms is nothing less than shameful. By leaving out crucial facts (or emasculating them beyond recognition), the media can help dictate how the public views the issues. Some examples:

- Kennesaw and crime. On January 11, 1984, the Associated Press carried an unfavorable story about Kennesaw, Georgia — a city that in 1982 passed a law requiring residents to possess firearms. What was the story about? The fact that in 1984, Kennesaw was the only city in its county with an increase in crime during the past year. The point of the story was obvious: Lawful ownership of guns doesn't deter crime.

  Unfortunately, the reporter didn't tell the whole story.

  Sure, violent crimes increased from one crime in 1982 to three in 1983. But the year before the pro-gun law was enacted, there were 17 violent crimes in the city! If anything, the record showed a huge net decrease in violent crime since the law was enacted. Further, the reporter also neglected to mention that in 1983 the number of residential burglaries continued to fall dramatically. There were 55 residential burglaries in 1981, 19 in 1982, and only nine in 1983.

- Morton Grove and crime. In October 1982, a Scripps-Howard reporter filed an article about Morton Grove, the city that banned handguns in the early 1980s. The article set out to debunk the predictions that a crime wave would follow passage of the ban. The reporter showed that such predictions were false because no crime wave had yet occurred in Morton Grove. What he didn't mention was the fact that few people were paying attention to the ban. they simply disregarded it. Only about 17 handguns had been turned into the police at that time!

- Proposition 15. In 1982, Californians defeated the anti-gun referendum, Proposition 15. Standard media analysis was that they "gun lobby" simply bought the election. It was generally claimed that the "gun lobby" outspent gun-control proponents three to one. Here again was another distortion. The "facts" may have been correct; but the context was not.

As sociology professor William Tonso points out: "[T]hese media analysts seldom mention that while the opponents of the proposition had to purchase media time and space to promote their position, the pro-control forces had the almost unanimous free support of the California major media and even some free support from the national media. As University of Illinois sociologist David Bordua has noted, the 15-minute pro-gun control segment of 60 Minutes that aired nine days before the Proposition 15 vote alone would have cost about $6 million at that program's going advertising rate. Opponents of the proposition spent a total of about $6 million to defeat the measure."

NBC Today Show. Weatherman Willard Scott has used his "Constitution Minutes" to argue that the right to own and bear arms "is not guaranteed to all citizens by the Constitution." The Second Amendment, according to Scott, was intended to "provide for an effective militia," and to "prevent the federal government from disarming your state's National Guard" — not to "give every citizen the right to go duck hunting." Mr. Scott would do better to stay a weatherman and not try to masquerade his ignorance as constitutional scholarship.

Sometimes the distortions on the part of the media reach gutter level. An editorial cartoonist for the *Arkansas Democrat,* for example, drew a cartoon that tried to tie John Hinckley to the National Rifle Association. On the left side of the cartoon was a grandmother, holding a trophy for marksmanship in one hand and a gun in the other. The caption from her mouth reads: "I'm the NRA." On the right side of the cartoon was John Hinckley. The words coming out of his mouth: "So am I." In making this sleazy cartoon, the cartoonist had blithely ignored the fact that Hinckley is not an NRA member. The newspaper finally retracted the libelous cartoon after being contacted by NRA attorneys. But the illustration never should have been printed to begin with.

Another example of such yellow journalism occurred during the multiple murders in Palm Bay, Florida in April, 1987. Writes Paul Blackman: "Before the news media even had a name for the suspect, both the Associated Press and United Press International wire services were falsely reporting that the gunman was an NRA member. That libel was reported widely in both the print and electronic media with virtually no newspaper, radio or television station so much as seeking to verify the information with the NRA. And, almost none of the media ever bothered to correct the serious error."

[Calling the Shots, The Gun Grabbers, and Gun Control and the National Magazine Media, "Mugged by the Media," in the *American Rifleman,* June 1987)]

Plastic Guns

Recently, there's been virtual hysteria about so-called "plastic" handguns. Politicians and news reporters have seized this issue and are running with it, spreading lies, rumors, and misinformation in the process. They charge that plastic handguns easily evade airport detection systems, whereas other normal guns cannot. They claim that plastic guns are being manufactured primarily for use by terrorists.

They're wrong.

It's simply incredible how much false information has been circulated in such a short time. The public is being duped.

So what are the facts about these new guns?

The Glock 17

The initial uproar about plastic guns concerned the Austrian firearm called the Glock 17. The Glock is the official pistol of the Austrian Army; it is also a NATO standard pistol. ["The Glock 17," *American Rifleman*, May 1986.]

But there's one thing that the Glock is not: all-plastic. Its outer casing is non-metal. But overall, the Glock is about 83% steel. To be exact, it contains 19 ounces of steel and 4 ounces of lead. That's 23 ounces of metal in a 24 ounce gun!

With this much metal, the Glock-17 is hardly less detectable than other firearms.

The Associate Director of the Bureau of Alcohol, Tobacco, and Firearms has confirmed this. In testimony before Congress, he termed many public reports on the Glock 17 "wildly inaccurate." He further stated: "There is nothing inherent in the Glock that would assist anyone in smuggling it, and ammunition for it, in a usable fashion through properly maintained x-ray and magnetometer screening such as that currently used for security purposes. Similarly, there is nothing about the Glock, disassembled, that should make it harder to detect, in a usable fashion, than any number of readily available firearms using more conventional materials. In this regard, the issue is not one of the firearm itself, so much as it is the alertness of security personnel." [Testimony of Phillip C. McGuire, Associate Director (Law Enforcement), Bureau of Alcohol, Tobacco and Firearms, before the Subcommittee on Crime, U.S. House of Representatives, May 15, 1986, pp. 1-2, emphasis added.]

Still unconvinced? The leading manufacturer of x-ray scanners for the nation's airports has come out with a photograph which shows that the Glock can be detected. The photo is an unretouched picture taken from an x-ray monitor machine. It shows a full briefcase containing a Glock 17 — which is readily visible. "Who says we can't stop the Glock?" reads the ad. It continues: "There have been reports that the 'plastic' Glock 17 automatic pistol can't be detected by present airport security methods. Since 92% of the x-ray security systems installed in United States airports are Linescan units (made by Astrophysics) we feel compelled to respond to these reports."

"The Linescan X-ray Security System has no difficulty in detecting metal guns and plastics in airports, correctional institutions, customs facilities, nuclear power plants, and corporate mailrooms around the world."

Despite all of this, there is a severe problem with the detection systems at our airports. But as the

Associate Director of the BATF mentioned, this problem has little to do with guns like the Glock-17. It has much to do with obsolete equipment and poorly trained operators. Much of the equipment in use relies heavily on its human operators — operators are notorious for not noticing the most basic of weapons. Under the current system even conventional, completely metal guns can often escape detection. This problem has existed for some time. It hasn't been created by the mostly-metal, partly "plastic" Glock-17.

["The Glock 17," *American Rifleman*, May 1986]

The Real Plastic Gun

Of course, the Glock-17 isn't the end of the story. It isn't any less detectable than conventional firearms because it is still mostly metal. But what about truly non-metal guns? What happens if they are developed? Won't these guns truly be "undetectable" and therefore highly dangerous?

They need not be. And it doesn't look like they will be. As of right now, the world's only gun that is almost all non-metal is the one being developed by Florida inventor David Byron. Except for a few metal springs, this gun will be made completely of high strength polymers and ceramics. Its weight will be only 3 1/2 ounces! But before you jump out of your seats in fright about terrorism, listen to this: This non-metal gun will be even more detectable than current metal guns.

That's because its inventor has developed a passive implant for the gun — an implant that would be placed so that it would be impossible to remove without destroying the gun itself. The implant would set off an alarm in a warning detector that has been developed. The detectors are cheap and can be installed "virtually overnight" according to the gun's designer. The detectors will go off automatically if any one brings a gun with the implant within ten feet.

["World's First All-Plastic Pistol," *American Firearms Industry*, May 1986, pp. 18-19, 36.]

The Legislative Threat

This whole controversy has now moved to the political realm, with certain politicians trying to capitalize on current fears by enacting legislation. The problem is that the proposed legislation is so broad. And it won't work.

For example, members of the House of Representatives came up with at least two anti-plastic gun bills during 1986 that would have restricted virtually every existing gun. Phillip McGuire, the associate director for law enforcement at the BATF, said this about the two bills:

"[E]xisting technology is such that language in both bills could create serious problems, not for the terrorist, but for the legitimate firearms industry and for enforcers of the law.

"For example, Mr. Biaggi's draft refers to a nonmetal firearm as one 'substantially constructed' of plastic of other nonmetal material. That definition covers almost every existing rifle and shotgun in commerce and almost any handgun using rubber, wood, or plastic oversized grips. Under the same bill, a licensed gunsmith who affixes a custom fiberglass stock or oversized wooden grips to a firearm, and removes some metal to accommodate the change, may well have made a weapon that has a 'diminished susceptibility to detection by airport metal detectors or other security devices.' Certainly, reducing barrel length within legal limits diminishes the overall metal mass, and arguable the detectability of a firearm. Yet this is a fairly common practice.

"H.R. 4194 focuses on the concept of 'readily detectable...by standard security equipment commonly used at airports' without outlining what either 'readily detectable' or 'standard' imply. Hypothetically, an all nonmetal firearm would be of sufficient mass and density to be readily detectable by x-ray equipment generally in use now. Similarly, the term 'readily identifiable as a firearm' in H.R. 4194 is also unclear. Such items as pen or cane guns are already subject to the provisions of Title II of the Gun Control Act. As such they are already subject to tight controls... With regard to other types of firearms, I think we would quickly find this entirely too subjective a standard to effectively regulate and enforce." (emphasis added) [McGuire, Subcommittee on Crime, U.S. House of Representatives, May 15, 1986, pp. 3-4.]

The Real Danger and the Real Problem

We all need to be concerned with terrorism. But the proposals by politicians like Biaggi to ban plastic handguns are insane. Banning plastic handguns would be the worst thing we could do! Such a measure would only give us a false sense of security. As we all should know from the failure of Prohibition, banning something doesn't eliminate its availability. Whether plastic handguns are legal or not, if terrorists want them, they will get them. The opportunistic politicians who suggest otherwise are either hopelessly naive or consciously lying.

At best, then, plastic handgun bans evade the issue. David Byron, the Florida inventor of the all-"plastic" handgun, explains:

"The hysteria over plastic guns masks the real problem: the woefully inadequate state of weapons detection in the United States. This weapons detection grid, our first line of defense against terrorists, was designed to find weapons of a type developed 80 years ago and is dependent on fallible human operators.

"Weapons now in the terrorist arsenal include composite assassination pistols designed by the Soviets to sneak through airports and embassy gates, Soviet plastic hand grenades the size of golf balls that are small enough to carry in the mouth, and plastic explosives — of which Libya has 40,000 pounds! Remember, only a couple of pounds of plastic explosive were used to murder 329 people aboard an Air India jet two years ago.

"To make matter worse, even conventional metal guns and grenades can easily make their way past our detectors, as reported by the Federal Aviation Administration recently."

What we really need, then, is better airport detection systems and stiffer penalties for terrorists. If legislators really want to fight terrorism, they should support the modernization of detection equipment at airports — and legislate a mandatory death penalty for anyone who participates in the skyjacking of an airplane.

Hope for the Future

New technologies will make it even easier in the future for us to detect everything from plastic explosives to non-metal guns. For example, there is the "Low-z" x-ray system. According to a staff paper put out by Congress's Office of Technology Assessment, this system "offers unique capabilities and could potentially be very useful in inspection of packages or baggage containing plastic firearms or plastic explosives. Other technologies may also prove useful."

David Byron explains further:

"The FAA in recent congressional testimony talked of vapor detectors and infrared imaging devices now being tested that can detect both conventional and plastic weapons, and which may automate the procedure so there is less reliance on human operators. After the Air India disaster, Canada adopted explosive vapor detectors that can pick up explosives and ammunition, and there is now a bill before Congress to upgrade our detector grid."

[Staff paper, Technical Questions Regarding Plastic Firearms, Congress of the United States, Office of Technology Assessment, April, 1986; "Hysteria over plastic guns masks the real problem," by David Byron, *Orlando Sentinel*, June 25, 1987]

The Police and Guns

Policemen and their associations almost uniformly support gun rights. Consider the following statements from four major law-enforcement associations:

- The National Sheriffs' Association. "There is no valid evidence whatsoever to indicate that depriving law-abiding American citizens of the right to own arms would in any way lessen crime or criminal activity... The National Sheriffs' Association unequivocally opposes any legislation that has as its intent the confiscation of firearms... or the taking away from law-abiding American citizens their right to purchase, own, and keep arms."

- The American Federation of Police. "There are many Americans who fear for their lives. They know that often they will have to protect themselves, their own families, and their own property. Should these people be disarmed? There are enough laws. No, we don't need to disarm our loyal citizens, our friends, and our neighbors. We just need judges with the guts to make the use of a gun in a crime a risk that few will undertake in the future."

- The National Police Officers' Association of America: "We feel that an American citizen of voting age and good character should have the right to purchase without restriction a handgun, pistol, revolver, rifle, shotgun, or like item without interference by a government body."

The Views of Rank and File Policemen

There is also a considerable body of evidence that rank and file policemen overwhelmingly oppose gun control. Let me cite a few of the polls conducted over the past several years.

A national study of police opinion conducted by the Boston Police Department in 1976 found that nearly 83% of the respondents opposed a ban on the private possession of handguns. Some 80% approved of the possession of handguns in the home or place of business. And 50% approved of the possession of handguns on the person for protection. Only 8% felt that the federal government should take the lead in imposing national registration and licensing requirements. This survey included the opinions of the nation's highest ranking officers, including the chiefs of the 50 state police agencies and county sheriffs whose forces exceed 200 officers.

It is interesting to note that this poll was commissioned by Boston Police Chief Robert diGrazia, an outspoken advocate of gun control.

There was another major poll in 1977: The Crime Control Research Project survey, sponsored by the Second Amendment Foundation in conjunction with the American Law Enforcement Officers Association. Some 34,000 questionnaires were distributed to police chiefs, sheriffs, and street officers throughout the country. The GMA Research corporation approved the methodology of the poll and analyzed and verified the results.

According to this poll, more than 86% of those surveyed indicated that if they were an ordinary citizen, they would keep a firearm for the protection of their family and property.

More than 95% of those officers surveyed indicated that if a federal law were enacted banning private ownership of handguns, organized crime would continue to make such weapons available to the common criminal.

More than 83% of those policemen surveyed felt that criminals rather than citizens would benefit most from the banning of handguns.

Nearly 64% of those surveyed believed that an armed citizenry serves as a deterrent to crime.

Still another poll took place in August, 1980. Law Enforcement News, a publication of the Criminal Justice Center of the John Jay College of Criminal Justice surveyed its readers on the issue of gun control.

82% of the responding street officers said that local and state gun control ordinances do not help to reduce crime. They showed a similarly skeptical attitude toward stronger federal firearms legislation, according to Law Enforcement News.

The Police and McClure-Volkmer

Recently with the passage of the Firearms Owners Protection Act (McClure-Volkmer), there has been a resurgence of the myth that policemen support gun control. Quoting a handful of police officials, the media have made it appear that the police were against the bill. Nothing could be further from the truth! The heads of both the National Association of Chiefs of Police and the American Federation of Police endorsed McClure-Volkmer. Further, a survey they sent out to every police chief, every sheriff, and all federal and state police heads in the United States showed that they also supported the bill.

Conducted in 1986, this most recent survey explained that McClure-Volkmer allowed a law-abiding citizen to purchase a firearm in another state and place it in the locked trunk of his car and then take it back home without fear of breaking the law. Police officials were asked if they felt that law-abiding citizens should be allowed to do this. Eighty-seven percent responded yes.

The poll also produced other results bearing on the question of gun ownership:

- 93% of the respondents said that it has been their experience that criminals get their guns illegally instead of from licensed gun dealers.

- 98% felt that law-abiding citizens have the right to own and purchase a firearm for home or business protection.

- 89% thought that gun control laws like New York's "Sullivan Act" don't have an effect on criminals.

- 91% didn't agree that gun bans or severe restrictions on guns have an effect on reducing gun crimes. [*Gun Week*, July 4, 1986]

How Some Police Promote Handguns to Stop Crime

Some police departments across the country have actually advocated citizen purchases of handguns in order to reduce crime. Some examples:

Miami, Florida. In the wake of the 1980 riots, the Miami policemen's association advised citizens to buy guns to defend themselves, "because we can't do it for you."

Orlando, Florida. A few years ago, faced with an epidemic of rapes, the police department sponsored a highly-publicized course in handgun self-defense for women. In the nine months following the program, there were just three rapes — a 90 percent reduction! The general crime rate also decreased.

Highland Park, Michigan. When merchants angrily demanded action from police in the wake of a series of armed robberies and murders, the police ran a high-profile firearms training course for storeowners. During the four months prior to the course, there were 190 holdups. In the four months following after training, there were none.

Those Police Who Don't Support Guns

Though the overwhelming majority of policemen don't support gun control, there are a few. The media love to quote them as representing the "police" view on gun restrictions. But they are hardly representative of the majority of police. Consider the background of some of the key anti-gun "policemen," as provided by Massad F. Ayoob. Ayoob is a former contributing editor of Law and Order and now feature editor of Trooper. Ayoob is himself a former policeman — he carried a badge for eight years. He has been named the International Director of Firearms Training for the Defensive Tactics Institute.

Anti-Gun Police:

Patrick Murphy.

> Murphy served as police commissioner of New York City. He has attacked America's police as being stupid, unprofessional, under-educated and provincial. He has been expelled from one major police chiefs' group, and many members of the International Association of Chiefs of Police consider him an enemy of everything they stand for.

Robert diGrazia.

> Mr. diGrazia served as top cop for Boston and Montgomery County, Maryland before being fired from the latter post, reportedly due in part to his having totally alienated the patrol force under him and shattered department morale. Today, he advertises in legal journals as an expert witness available to testify against policemen — an action to which his peers, the members of the International Association of Chiefs of Police, have responded with utter disgust.

John Buckley.

> Buckley is a former sheriff of Middlesex County, Massachusetts. He is prominent among the so-called law enforcement leaders against gun ownership, capital punishment, etc. The post of sheriff that Buckley filled was an elected one; he was in charge of jail administration and the service of legal papers. In other words, he was fairly far removed from the reality of street crime. Buckley recently stated on a TV talk show that he had never carried a gun.

A closing comment about those police who support gun control. Says Jim Cirillo, who served 23 years with the New York City Police Department and then joined the U.S. Customs Service: "It's my experience that any policemen who tells you he's in favor of gun control is a small-minded guy who probably works in an office instead of on the street. When you understand what's happening out there, you know gun control is meaningless. New York has always had the toughest gun laws in the country, but the people we went up against always had them. Hell, if they were ready to rob and kill people, what did they care about getting bootlegged or stolen guns to do it with?"

[*Gun Week*, July 4, 1986, The Rights of Gun Owners, The Police View of Gun Control.]`1

Product Liability

Guns are at the center of an increasingly bizarre chapter in American jurisprudence. In essence, lawyers are trying to sue gun manufacturers for the criminals misuse of their products. So if a robber shoots a bank teller, these lawyers want the banks teller to sue the gun maker!

This is an incredible abrogation of the idea of personal responsibility. Just think of it — penalizing gun makers for crimes instead of criminals! This is despite the fact that the vast majority of guns owned aren't involved in criminal activities. They are used for self-protection, hunting, recreation, or other legitimate purposes.

The idea that manufacturers can be held liable for the misuse of their products is not only absurd, it's frightening. Just think of the legal consequences if we applied this principle across the board. The ramifications have been discussed by Nicholas Calio and Donald Santarelli of the Washington Legal Foundation:

"The principle, once established, will be applicable to other products for which the risk of intentional misuse can only be reduced or eliminated by impairing or destroying the product's functionality.

"For instance, the proposed theory could be applied to products such as knives, alcohol, drugs, cigarettes, and automobiles to name a few. Knives are involved in incidents of violent crime at a rate which almost equals that of all firearms, not just handguns. Alcohol is implicated in more homicides and other violent crimes than all firearms combined. Cigarette misuse is involved in the majority of fire-related deaths and injuries at a rate which is statistically significant in relation to the number of handgun-related deaths. Finally, automobile misuse accounts for a far greater number of injuries and deaths every year than do handguns and all other firearms."

[Turning the Gun on Tort Law: Aiming At Courts To Take Products Liability To The Limit, by Donald E. Santarelli and Nicholas Calio (Washington Legal Foundation, Washington, D.C. : 1982)]

Who's Doing It

One of the key law firms fighting for this insane legal position is Windle Turley, P.C., Attorneys and Counselors. Turley is a Dallas law firm, and as detailed in my recent book "The Gun Grabbers," it has fired off a "barrage of lawsuits aimed at making handgun manufacturers liable for the damage inflicted by their weapons."

Here are two examples:

- In 1977, 15-year-old Ken Hacker accidentally shot a classmate, who was left paralyzed. Turley sued the companies who had made and sold the gun that was used.

- Jim Patterson was shot and killed with a revolver by a would-be robber at a Dallas 7-Eleven store. Turley sued for $500,000 in damages against the gun's manufacturer.

All told, the Windle Turley firm has filed over 80 product liability suits against handguns.

Fortunately, none that have come to trial have succeeded. Yet.

Why the Suits Might Succeed

The sad fact is, one of these days Turley or someone else may succeed in what they're trying to do. The courts have already accepted the idea that companies can be sued for the misuse of their products. Journalist John G. West, Jr. explains:

"It is the criminal justice fiasco all over again. During the 1950s and 60s, reformist lawyers and social workers sought to blame crime on society rather than on criminals. Criminals obtained light sentences and 'rehabilitation,' while society suffered under the load of expensive social programs designed to eliminate the 'root causes' of crime. Today, civil lawyers are similarly seeking to blame corporations for the injuries caused by the abuse of their products.

"And these lawyers are succeeding. The list of judicial horror stories grows longer each year.

"In 1979, for example, Business Week reported about a teenager who doused the burning wick of a candle in Faberge perfume — in order to 'scent' the candle. Unsurprisingly, 'the perfume ignited, burning a friend's neck. Claiming that Faberge had failed to warn consumers of the perfume's flammability, the friend won a $27,000 judgement. Despite its argument that there was no way to foresee that someone would pour perfume onto an open flame, Faberge lost its appeal.

"If this seems ridiculous, consider the effort underway by gun control lawyers to hold gun manufacturers liable for crimes committed with handguns.

"In October 1985, the highest state court in
Maryland held that producers, distributors and
retailers of 'Saturday Night Specials' should be
liable for injuries cause by their use in crimes."

What Lawyers are Saying

It's interesting — and disturbing — to read what
product liability lawyers themselves are saying about
the cases they are filing. Some seem to want a legal
free-for-all.

In the August 1984 issue of Case and Comment, for
example, lawyer Edward Swartz chided his brethren
for failing "to recognize several cases each year that
could result in very large hazardous case recoveries.
Although this is a very lucrative area of law, most
general practitioners have not had time to keep up
with the new theories and approaches that turn
lackluster fact patterns into million-dollar verdicts
and settlements."

"Often lawyers miss these opportunities," wrote
Swartz, "because they fail to approach the case from
the proper perspective. They query whether the injured
party was at fault, instead of looking to the
manufacturer, marketer, retailer, or designer of the
culprit product... For example, when children are
horribly burned and disfigured after flammable
bedding or clothing ignites or when a child is severely
brain damaged after ingesting a small toy, they might
query,'Why weren't the parents more vigilant?' These
questions and others like them represent a
fundamentally flawed approach to many product—
related personal injury cases." (emphasis added)

Swartz later conceded that "carelessness is a
problem," but according to him, "it's often the
manufacturer's problem, not the victim's."

The Solution

There is no question that this "blame the business"
mentality has been a major reason that product

liability lawsuits — and insurance rates — have skyrocketed. (In less than a decade, product liability actions lodged in federal court have jumped over 500 percent!)

The chaos has sent Congress and various state legislatures scrambling to come up with legislative packages to deal with the liability problem. Unfortunately, many proposed solutions focus on side issues. But anything that helps put the lid on corporate liability lawsuits will bode well for those who support gun rights. The less support given to the idea that you can sue companies on the basis of product misuse the better.

Public Opinion

Gun control advocates often claim that the public overwhelmingly supports their drive to rid the nation of guns. And indeed, when people are asked by pollsters whether or not they favor "gun control," the vast majority say yes.

But that's only part of the story.

According to the major polls on the subject, the vast majority of Americans also believe that we have a Constitutional right to own guns. They also think that gun control won't keep guns out of the hands of criminals. And they are against a ban on handguns.

So what's going on here? How can the same people support gun control and gun rights simultaneously? Well, part of this disparity is created by the muddled meaning of the phrase "gun control." "Gun control" means all sorts of different things to different people.

Some think that punishing criminals who use guns in a crime is gun control. Still others think that nothing less than a gun ban is true gun control. So when a pollster asks people whether or not they support "gun control," he is really asking several questions at once. Those who answer the question"yes." do so for a multitude of reasons.

So simply saying that most Americans support "gun control" is a meaningless statement. The question is : What type of gun control do they support?

The Evidence of Public Opinion Polls

There are two major surveys dealing with the issue of guns. Both were national surveys conducted in 1978; both were comprehensive in the questions that they asked. One was commissioned for the NRA; the other was done for the anti-gun Center for the Study and Prevention of Handgun Violence.

The pro-gun survey was conducted by the firm Decision/Making Information (DMI). The DMI survey was based on a sample of 1500 registered voters. Its findings?

- 89% of registered voters believe that the Constitution of the United States gives them the right to keep and bear arms.

- 87% of registered voters would oppose a law giving police the power to decide who may or may not own a firearm.

- 91% of registered voters agree that the registration of handguns will not prevent criminals from acquiring or using them for illegal purposes.

- 93% of registered voters agree that anyone having a gun while committing a violent crime should receive a severe and mandatory prison sentence.

The major anti-gun survey was conducted in 1978 by Cambridge Research Associates (CRA). It was based on a sample of U.S. adults (not just registered voters). Here are some of the CRA findings:

- 51% of American adults oppose banning all private ownership of handguns. 18% are neutral on the matter.

- 62% of American adults oppose using public funds to buy back and destroy existing handguns on a mandatory basis.

- 58% of American adults oppose banning the future sale of all handguns.

- 78% of American adults agree with the statement, "Gun control laws affect only law-abiding citizens, criminals will always be able to find guns."

Limitations of CRA Poll

According to the CRA poll, however, large majorities of Americans also support things like handgun licensing, handgun registration, waiting periods for criminal record checks, and mandatory prison sentences for those using guns in a crime.

But one must carefully analyze these findings to find out what they really mean. Some of these so-called "gun control" measures that the majority of Americans support are also supported readily by the pro-gun movement.

For example, pro-gun groups readily support mandatory sentences for those criminals who use guns in violent crimes.

As for the supposed wide support for gun registration and licensing, this must be taken with a grain of salt. Other polls clearly indicated that the vast majority of Americans also believe that they have the right to own a gun if they want to. So it is hard to believe that they would simultaneously support measures such as licensing which would restrict that right. It must be concluded, then, that people support licensing and registration only because they think that these measures won't impair their own ability to purchase guns.

But anyone who has studied the matter knows that this is not the case. Gun registration and licensing laws do curtail the ability of honest people to get guns for self-defense and other lawful reasons. Just look at what's happening in New York! Under New York's licensing system, it is virtually impossible to get the police to issue you a gun permit. It doesn't matter how law-abiding you are! Once the American public learns the facts about gun licensing and registration, it will no doubt oppose such measures.

More Recent Polls

Although 1978 was the last time a comprehensive gun poll was conducted, there have been numerous recent surveys that have asked questions relevant to gun rights.

In 1984, an Associated Press poll asked people whether they had started carrying a gun or other weapon to protect themselves from crime. Some 10% of respondents indicated that they had.

In 1983, a Gallup poll asked people about the effects of stricter handgun laws. 31% of the people thought that stricter laws would not reduce the number of crimes very much; 25% more thought that stricter gun laws wouldn't reduce the number of crimes at all. 43% of the people thought that stricter laws wouldn't reduce the number of people killed by guns in family arguments very much or at all. 43% of the people thought that stricter gun laws wouldn't even reduce the number of accidental deaths very much or at all.

In 1985, a Gallup poll revealed that 56% of the American public oppose laws banning the sale and possession of handguns.

In 1985, an ABC-*Washington Post* revealed that 69% of America's gun owners said that if a burglar broke into their house of apartment during the night, they thought that they would use their gun.

[Sourcebook of Criminal Justice Statistics, 1985, pp. 194-196, 200-201.]

In 1987, the *Chicago Sun-Times* sponsored a scientific survey of Chicago area residents that showed substantial grass-roots support for guns. 63% of the people in the area supported the right of handgun ownership in the home for self protection.

Handgun ownership won most support in Chicago itself, which has a higher crime rate than surrounding areas. The city went for handguns 69% to 31%.
[*Gun Week*, May 22, 1987, p. 11]

Data Other than Polls

Of course, polls are certainly not the only way to gauge public opinion. Indeed, they aren't necessarily the best way to judge informed public opinion. Perhaps the best way to find out what the informed public thinks is to analyze election results — for voters are much more likely to be informed about the issues that they are voting on than non-voters are.

In the area of elections, the gun rights side wins hands down. Voters have repeatedly defeated efforts to curtail gun liberties.

In 1976, voters in Massachusetts rejected a ban on the possession of handguns by 2 to 1.

In 1982, California voters defeated a state initiative that would have required the registration of all existing handguns and would have banned the sale, manufacture or importation of any new handguns. On the positive side, voters in New Hampshire, Nevada and Idaho have all added strong "right to keep and bear arms" causes to their state constitutions in recent years.

[Under the Gun, Firearms and Violence, Seven Myths of Gun Control]

Racism and Guns

Anti-gun activists love to portray gun control as a "liberal" and "progressive" cause. However, the history behind the gun control movement puts it in a completely different light.

Gun Control is Anti-Black

Some of the first American gun control laws were those enacted to keep Southern blacks defenseless and in subjugation. Before the Civil War, slave codes barred both slaves and free blacks from owning arms — except under extremely narrow circumstances. After the war, the slave codes reappeared as "black codes." Once again, the right of arms was denied to blacks. Congress was so enraged that it passed the 15th Amendment to nullify such statutes. Southern states then ingeniously circumvented the Amendment by banning all but the most expensive handguns — thus placing handgun ownership out of the average black's reach. [That Every Man Be Armed, Stephen Halbrook; "Gun Control: White Man's Law," by William Tonso.]

Today, proposals to ban so-called "Saturday Night Specials" are merely a rehash of the black codes in the South. The ostensible purpose of banning such cheap handguns is because they are more likely to be used in crime. But according to prominent sociologists James Wright and Peter Rossi, banning cheap "Saturday Night Specials" might actually promote more handgun deaths. This is because criminals could substitute higher caliber handguns for the cheaper, lower caliber guns that have been banned. And higher caliber guns are intrinsically more accurate. In other words, criminals would be less likely to miss you when they shoot. [Under the Gun, p. 203]

An even more fundamental effect, however, of banning cheap handguns would be to disarm poor people. Ban cheap handguns and only the rich will be able to afford protection.

Because of these things, some black leaders are now coming out against gun control. One of these is Detroit resident General Laney. Mr. Laney is the force behind the National Black Sportsman's Association. His opinion of gun control? "Gun control is really race control. People who embrace gun control are really racists in nature. All gun laws have been enacted to control certain classes of people, mainly black people, but the same laws used to disarm blacks are being used to disarm white people as well." [Gun Control: White Man's Law, p. 1]

Gun Control and Immigrants

But blacks aren't the only ones who have been the targets of gun control laws. At the turn of the century, gun control in the North was spurred by anti-immigrant hysteria. Under New York's Sullivan Law, for example, Southern and Eastern European immigrants found it virtually impossible to legally own guns — because the police would rarely issue them permits. [William Tonso, sociology professor at University of Evansville (Indiana), Gun Control: White Man's Law]

Self Defense

In a world like this, you can't just bury your head in the sand and hope everything will turn out all right. You can't just expect the police to protect you — for more often than not, they won't be there when you need them. You must be ready to defend yourself.

That brings us to the handgun.

Hated, berated, slammed, and damned, handguns have been given a bum rap. Gun control advocates like to spread the myth that handguns don't really help save lives; that they really aren't very good for self-protection. They're wrong.

The Effectiveness of Handguns

Handguns provide one of the most effective methods of preventing you from becoming just another crime statistic. Consider the results of a report issued during the 1970's about robberies in Chicago:

- Among those victims using handguns in self-defense, 66% of them were successful in warding off the attack and keeping their property.

- Among those victims using non-gun weapons, only 40% were successful.

- Among those victims fleeing the scene, only 35% were successful.

- Among those victims invoking physical force, only 35% were successful.

* Among those using verbal shouting, only 20% were successful.

Handguns are likely to become an even more effective tool as result of a recent trend in robberies and aggravated assaults.

An average of 1.2 million people each year face a robber, with over half of the victims physically attacked.

From 1974 to 1984, however, firearms use in robberies fell steadily. In 1974, 45% of robberies were carried out with firearms. By 1985, only about 35% of robberies were carried out with firearms.

The same trend is occurring with aggravated assaults. In 1974 firearms were used in about 25% of all aggravated assaults; a decade later they were used in 21% of aggravated assaults.

The bottom line of these statistics is that you are now more likely to face a robber who is either not armed at all, or not armed with a firearm. So if you have a firearm, the balance will be decidedly in your favor.

Of course, unless you can get a permit to carry a concealed weapon, you won't be able to have a firearm on you if the attack is on the street.

Nevertheless, it would still be beneficial to own a firearm for self-defense in the home, for substantial numbers of violent crimes continue to be perpetrated in people's residences. In 1983, for example, 37% of all rapes and attempted rapes occurred in the home (that figure fell to 26% in 1984). In 1984, 19% of all robberies resulting in serious assault also occurred there; so did 19% of all aggravated assaults resulting in injury.

Because of the many crimes taking place in the home, a gun at your residence may very well save your life.

[Sourcebook of Criminal Justice Statistics, 1985, pp. 264, 383-384, 388; *Gun Week*, April 24, 1987, p. 1; Statistical Abstract of the United States, 1987, p. 161.]

Further evidence that guns are useful in self-defense was provided by "The Armed Criminal in America," a

1985 report for the National Institute of Justice by James Wright and Peter Rossi. The study survey over 1,800 convicts currently serving prison sentences in 10 states. According to the report:

- 56% of the convicts agreed that "a criminal is not going to mess around with a victim he knows is armed with a gun."

- 81% agreed that "a smart criminal always tries to find out if his potential victim is armed."

- 57% agreed that "most criminals are more worried about meeting an armed victim than they are about running into the police."

- 74% agreed that "one reason burglars avoid houses when people are at home is that they fear being shot during the crime."

- And 58% agreed that "a store owner who is known to keep a gun on the premises is not going to get robbed very often." [*Point Blank*, April 1987, p. 2]

In short, the evidence shows that if you want to defend yourself against attack, the gun is the method to use. And people do use them to protect themselves.

Gun Use for Self-Defense

According to a Media General/Associated Press poll in 1984, 44% of Americans keep a gun at home to protect themselves from crime. Other polls suggest a somewhat smaller figure, but whatever the actual number, one thing is emphatically clear: Gun ownership is one of the most popular methods of crime prevention in the nation. By comparison, only 25% of Americans have engraved their valuables with an identifying number; only seven percent of the people have a burglar alarm; and only seven percent of Americans have joined a neighborhood watch program. [Sourcebook of Criminal Justice Statistics, 1985, p. 193; Statistical Abstract of the United States, 1987, p. 160.]

Further, according to a poll conducted in 1978, 13 million registered voters live in households where a family member has had to use a gun in self-defense.

According to the same poll, over five million voters or their families had actually fired a gun for self-protection. [Under the Gun, p. 147]

Another 1978 poll, this one done for Milton Eisenhower's Center for the study of Handgun Violence, projected that 300,000 Americans a year use handguns to deter criminals. Other projections by scholars suggest that the number is closer to 600,000 — or more.

In 1985, an ABC-*Washington Post* poll asked gun owners whether they thought they would use their firearms if a burglar broke into their house or apartment during the night. Some 69% of those polled said that they would. [Sourcebook of Criminal Justice Statistics, 1985, p. 195]

Case Examples of Self-Defense

But the statistics hardly tell the whole story. They are cold and abstract. The stories of those who have used handguns in self-defense are not. Consider some examples:

- Chicago, Illinois, May 1986. A would-be mugger picked the wrong victim on a Chicago subway. The 16-year-old pulled his gun on an off-duty Chicago police officer, who shot and killed the youth. Officer Frank Paluch said his "biggest mistake" was going into the subway "all dressed up" with his date. Paluch said he shot the youth because, "I knew he was going to shoot. I could sense it." Had he not been a policeman, Paluch would not have been allowed to have that handgun — and he and his date might be dead. [*Gun Week*, June 6, 1986, p. 2]

- Missoula, Montana, September, 1986: Doug Wells was clubbed unconscious and then bound by a man outside his home. The intruder then tied Wells' wife and dragged the 34-year-old gunsmith to the basement and stabbed him. The man went back upstairs, stopping Kirsten Wells from dialing for help, but then returned to check on Wells, who had freed himself and grabbed a rifle. Wells shot the man and, in the struggle, killed him. [*The Missoulian*, Missoula, Montana, 9/5/86]

• New Orleans, Louisiana, January 1987: Merchant Wayne Grass was leaving his store when a man accosted and tried to rob him at knife point. Grass reached into his truck, which was parked in front of the store, as his assailant tried to slash his throat. The owner was able to get his gun and shoot the attacker, killing him. The knife-wielder had recently been released from prison after serving a burglary sentence. [*The Times-Picayune*, New Orleans, La. 1/8/87]

• Tuscaloosa, Alabama, January 1987: Seeing a man enter his convenience store, the night manager noticed it was the same person who had robbed the store previously. The man picked up a few items and asked for a pack of cigarettes, then drew a butcher knife and told the store manager he was going to rob the store again. "No you're not," replied the manager as he pulled a .38 from his pocket. The would-be robber pleaded with the manager not to shoot him and then fled empty-handed. [*The News*, Tuscaloosa, AL. 1/2/87]

• Grandview, Washington, April, 1987: When T.C. Moore heard screaming near his farm, he grabbed his shotgun and went to investigate. He found as man attempting to rape a 15-year-old girl and fired several warning shots, halting the attack. The farmer held the would-be rapist for police [*The Herald*, Tri-Cities, Washington, 4/2/87]

The Laws about Self-Defense

Self-defense laws vary from state to state. In general, a gun owner may shoot a robber, mugger or housebreaker only to escape imminent and unavoidable danger of death or grave bodily harm. Some states actually require a victim to retreat — and only when his back is against a wall, can he shoot his life-threatening assailant.

Further, you must shoot only during the time of imminent danger — not after, not before. "The right of self-defense begins when danger begins, ends when the danger ends, and revives when he danger returns." [The Rights of Gun Owners, pp. 54-55]

For specific information on the self-defense laws in your state, check my book, The Rights of Gun Owners.

The Morality of Self Defense with Guns

Some people complain that it's not nice to shoot back at criminals. Well, it's not nice for criminals to victimize honest citizens either. Self-defense is an ancient, sacred right that has been upheld as just throughout the ages. Quotes on this subject from authorities ancient and modern follow:

"There exists a law, not written down anywhere but inborn in our hearts; a law which comes to us not by training or custom or reading but by derivation and absorption and adoption from nature itself; a law which has come to us not from theory but from practice, not by instruction but by natural intuition. I refer to the law which lays it down that, if our lives are endangered by plots or violence or armed robbers or enemies, any and every method of protecting ourselves is morally right." — Cicero.

"Civilized people are taught by logic, barbarians by necessity, communities by tradition; and the lesson is inculcated even in wild beasts by nature itself. They learn that hey have to defend their own bodies and persons and lives from violence of any and every kind by all the means within their power." — Cicero.

"He who thinks he is his own master, and has anything he may call his own, ought to have arms to defend himself and what he possess, or else he lives precariously and at discretion." — Andrew Fletcher, 17th century.

"Self-defense is a part of the law of nature; nor can it be denied the community, even against the king himself." — Barclay.
[That Every Man Be Armed, pp. 27, 17, 47, 29]

"In the early and mid-1970's, public advice was to cooperate with robbers and rapists in order to minimize personal injury. Appeasement, in other words. While this may be good advice under some circumstances, as general behavior it makes crime more rewarding. A nation of sheep is nice for wolves." — Morgan Reynolds, economist [Crime by Choice, p. 84]

"The whole subject of civilians carrying guns for self defense is discussed too much in the wrong places — ACLU cocktail parties, gun club gatherings — all placid atmospheres far removed from the terrifying reality of violent confrontation with the lawless. It should be discussed in prisons, where professional criminals are remarkably candid about their avoidance of armed citizens who can fight back. It should be discussed in rape crisis centers. Ask a woman who has been raped, whether she ever wished she had a gun when it happened... and whether she has bought one since. Her reply is likely to be 'yes' to at least the first, and often to both.

"Talk to the bereaved, who lost their loved ones to the violence of the streets. Talk to those who have been violated in their homes. Ask them how they feel about passive non-resistance. And when you have attuned yourself to the haunting fear that lives with them forever after their nightmare, you will be ready to talk with someone else who was in their place, but survived unscathed because they were armed.

"The contrast will be striking. These survivors don't put notches on their pistols, and they don't brag about what they had to do... The taking of a human life, no matter what the circumstances, is an unnatural act, an emotionally shattering experience that leaves its own scars forever. But none of those people regret what they did, and to a man, their first reaction was to go home to their wife and children and hug them, tightly and wordlessly." — Massad Ayoob [Armed and Alive]

Suicides and Guns

Gun control advocates often argue that the availability of guns makes it easier for people to commit suicide. They further contend that if guns were more harshly regulated that suicides would likely decrease.

Such charges are severely flawed.

No Positive Relationship

First off, it's just plain wrong to think that there is any positive relationship between guns and suicide rates. High gun ownership rates don't guarantee high suicide rates. And harsh gun control measures don't guarantee low suicide rates. These are facts.

Consider: Israel has one of the highest gun ownership rates in the world. According to the "guns promote suicides" hypothesis, it should have a commensurate suicide rate. It doesn't. In 1982, Israel's suicide rate was only 11.9 per 100,000 — less than the rates in countries with strict gun laws like Japan, Sweden and Britain.

Or let's look at it the other way around: Japan and Sweden both have tough anti-gun laws. So under the "gun control discourages suicides" hypothesis, they ought to have low suicide rates. They don't. Japan's suicide rate in 1982 was 34.4 people per 100,000; Sweden's was 35.2 per 100,000. The U.S.'s suicide rate, by comparison, was roughly 1/3 less — 23.7 per 100,000.

The Most Serious Flaw

Perhaps the most serious flaw in the arguments of gun controllers, however, is their implicit assumption that guns are the only easy way to commit suicide. Statistics show that fully 59% of suicides among women and 36% of successful suicides among men are done without firearms. Clearly, there are other ways to kill one's self than with a gun. Banning guns won't prevent suicides. If people intent on suicides can't get a gun on the black market, then they will simply use another method.

[The statistics cited here come from the Statistical Abstract of the United States, 1987, U.S. Bureau of the Census, Washington, D.C.]

Overestimating the Role of Guns

There's something else to remember here if we want to keep things in perspective. Gun control advocates rattle on as if guns are the most popular method to use in suicide attempts. Nothing could be further from the truth. Guns do play a role in suicides actually completed. But for every successful suicide there are from 8 to 10 suicide attempts. And in only about 3-6% of these attempts are guns used. In other words, guns are extremely unpopular among those who want to kill themselves. [Firearms and Violence, p. 168]

In conclusion, we should realize that the gun controllers are evading the real issue when they focus on guns in suicides. They muddy the waters and help draw us away from what we really ought to be doing. If we are truly interested in combating suicides — and we ought to be — we need to attack its root cause — family breakdowns, feelings of loneliness, feelings of unworthiness. Trying to attack guns instead is mere chicanery. This social problem is far too devastating to play political games with. Let's stop passing the buck onto an inanimate object.

Women's Rights

The right to live and be secure from personal attack is one of the most fundamental rights of human beings. Yet every year, thousands of women are denied this right.

For 1984 alone, it was estimated by the Department of Justice that women suffered over 160,000 rapes and attempted rapes, over 1.7 million assaults, and nearly 400,000 robberies.

That's not even mentioning the several thousand women who were murdered.

To put it another way: Every two hours another women is murdered; every 3 minutes a rape attempt occurs. [Sourcebook of Criminal Justice Statistics,1985.]

But if these statistics are horrifying, the personal examples they are built upon are even more so.

Consider some examples of the crimes that have been perpetrated in America in recent years.

Los Angeles, 1983. While walking through a park in a Los Angeles suburb, a 24-year-old woman was gang raped. While numerous residents in a nearby housing complex heard her cried for help, none went to her aid.

Washington, D.C. Three women were raped and brutally beaten for fourteen hours. Two of the women had telephoned the police shortly before the attack and were told help was on the way. It never came. The women sued the police department for negligence but lost. The Court of Appeals ruled that they couldn't sue the police.

In a world like this, where your fellow man may or may not help you, where the police may or may not respond, it is imperative that women take measures to defend themselves.

But how?

Methods of Self-Defense

There are various methods of self-protection. Some people promote martial arts training; others suggest tear-gas sprays, whistles and alarms. All these have major drawbacks.

Whistles and alarms. These are based on the premise that someone is nearby who will help you if they hear a sounding for help. This is a dangerous assumption to make.

Martial arts. It may take years for someone to become effective enough in the martial arts to ward off an attack. Even then, it is no guarantee. An assailant with a weapon (gun or otherwise) will still have the advantage. So will an assailant who is 100 pounds heavier than you.

Mace and Tear-Gas. You can't get the real thing. The chemicals sold to civilians are watered down versions. And they aren't very effective. As Massad Ayoob points out: "The Mace-type sprays have proven to be much less effective than once believed. Many people can take several streams of the stuff square in the face with no immediate ill effects. It only works right off when it's sprayed in the eyes, which is a no-no. Even that won't work if your assailant wears glasses, or shades. Drunks are almost immune." [In the Gravest Extreme, pp. 36-37]

What then will work?

Guns.

A Most Effective Defense

Handguns provide one of the most effective methods of preventing you from becoming just another crime statistic. Consider the results of a report issued during the 1970s about robberies in Chicago.

- Among those victims using handguns in self-defense, 66% of them were successful in warding off the attack and keeping their property.

- Among those victims using non-gun weapons, only 40% were successful.

- Among those victims fleeing the scene, only 35% were successful.

- Among those victims invoking physical force, only 22% were successful.

- Among those using verbal shouting, only 20% were successful.

In short, the evidence shows that if you want to defend yourself against attack, the handgun is the method to use. And people do use them to protect themselves. [Women's Views on Guns and Self-Defense, pp. 10-11]

Women who Fight Back

Fed up with being victimized by thugs, an increasing number of women are fighting back with guns. In a recent article titled "Targeting the Women's Market," *Newsday* told its readers about some of these women.

One of them is named Katharine; she lives with a female roommate in an apartment in Flushing, N.Y. Katharine bought a handgun because she was determined to defend herself. But it hasn't exactly been easy owning a gun. People have tried to discourage her from having it. "There are constant arguments that you get," she told *Newsday*. "I've gotten it from family, I've gotten it from friends, from strangers. Most people feel it's not going to happen to you. It happens to everyone else... I've never been one with the attitude that it only happens to other people. A woman living alone, two women living alone... when you come down to it, how do we defend ourselves? How do we stop somebody from giving [us] some sort of bodily harm? We can't. What the hell would I do with somebody who came in and said, 'I'm going to break your face,' at the least? Nothing." [*Gun Week,* June 13, 1986, p. 2]

But with a gun, she could do something.

Examples

Here are some stirring examples of how courageous women are defending themselves with guns:

- Atlanta, Georgia, January, 1982. Kathy Key fought four long minutes against a rapist, trying to get his throat, trying to kick him in the groin. There seemed to be nothing she could do. Suddenly, surprising even herself, Kathy realized she was clutching her shoulder bag. For a moment, she freed herself and fled for the kitchen as her assailant attempted to pull up his pants to pursue. She pulled her tiny derringer from her shoulder bag, and as Michael Narvaez put his arms around her again, she brought the derringer to his side. The only sound he made was a whisper. Two words: "Oh God." And then he was dead.

- Lancaster, Texas, July, 1986. A woman was loading a newspaper vending machine at 4 AM when a man approached her from behind and grabbed her by the neck. The attacker placed a piece of material around the woman's face and punched her, but she broke away and ran to her van. The 23-year-old woman pulled a .25 auto from her purse and shot her assailant three times. A wounded suspect was arrested minutes later. (*The Morning News,* Dallas, Texas, 7/19/87)

- Stockton, California, October, 1986. A woman awakened by a noise investigated and found a man coming through the back door of her home. She had armed herself with a pistol, and, when the man made a sexual remark, she told him to leave or she would shoot. The would-be rapist fled. (*The Record,* Stockton, California, 10/16/87)

Violent Crime and Guns

The most fundamental charge of those who advocate gun control is that guns somehow inherently promote crime. Thus, if we ban them or severely restrict them, crime will be reduced.

Or so the theory goes. The only problem with all this is reality. There is no significant empirical evidence to support the thesis that guns inherently promote crime.

Listen to the experts:

"There is little or no conclusive evidence to show that gun ownership among the larger population is, per se, an important cause of criminal violence." — James Wright, Peter Rossi, Kathleen Daly. Wright is Professor of Sociology at the University of Massachusetts, Amherst and directs the Social and Demographic Research Institute. Rossi is also Professor of Sociology at the University of Massachusetts, Amherst. A past director of the American Sociological Association, he has authored twenty books. Daly is Visiting Professor of Sociology at the State University of New York, Albany. [Under the Gun, p. 137]

"Virtually all of the evidence marshalled to established the association between gun ownership and violence could just as easily be interpreted as showing that more gun violence leads to more people acquiring guns for defensive purposes rather than the reverse." — Gary Kleck, Assistant Professor of Criminology at Florida State University. He has served as an

editorial consultant for the American Sociological
Review and as a grants consultant for the National
Science Foundation. [Firearms and Violence, p. 99]

"As the models and estimation techniques have
grown more sophisticated, the tendency has been to find
an inverse relationship between crime and gun
ownership rates — the higher gun ownership is, the
lower crime is, all equal." — Morgan O. Reynolds.
Reynolds is a professoɪ f Economics at Texas A & M
University. [Crime by Choice, p. 166]

There are various versions of the guns-cause-crime
argument. Here are two of the more popular ones with
rebuttals:

Version 1: Guns incite people to violence. They promote
aggression due to the learned association between guns
and violence.

Reply: There is little, if any, solid empirical evidence
to support this contention. At least four studies have
produced evidence that actually undercuts the 'guns
promote aggression' thesis. Of the three studies that
have produced findings in support of it, two were
conducted in Europe — in countries with cultures
significantly different than that of the United States.
It is questionable whether their findings can
legitimately be extrapolated to our population.
　　Further, one of the studies didn't even use guns as the
stimuli — it only used pictures of them! And its
measure of "aggression" was "the number of shocks
subjects said they wanted to give to the confederates
who had insulted them." Criminology Professor Gary
Kleck and Sociology Professor David Bordua point out
the problems with this: "The artificiality of these
conditions and the dubious validity of the aggression
measure makes the finding of questionable
generalizability."

Even beyond this, however, there is something else to consider. Regardless of whether or not guns can promote aggression in some people, at least two studies have shown that the presence of guns can also inhibit aggression. In short, people carrying guns can be inhibited by the feat of the consequences they will face if they assault someone else with a gun.

Considering all of the evidence, then, it seems that guns are as likely to inhibit violence as incite it. At least, that's what Criminology Professor Gary Kleck at Sociology Professor David Bordua think: The research findings "suggest that, for the population as a whole, guns are as likely to inhibit assaults as to incite them, and that gun ownership has no net effect on the frequently of assaults."

["Firearms and Firearms Regulation: Old Premises, New Research," Law and Policy Quarterly, July 1983 274-278.]

Version 2: Guns promote crime because they're so deadly. If people didn't have guns, then they'd use other weapons that aren't as deadly. Thus, crime fatalities would decrease.

Reply: Most gun control proposals are targeted only toward handguns — "Saturday Night Specials" in particular. It is extremely doubtful one could effectively ban such items (a black market would spring up immediately). Nevertheless, let us assume for the sake of argument that all handguns are effectively banned — an unlikely and extreme scenario, yet it is what most of the gun banners desire. Would such a ban decrease crime deaths?

To answer this question, one must estimate what weapons will be substituted by criminals for handguns. Will they turn to long guns? Or will they turn to knives? Even if only 30% of the criminals chose long guns (and the remaining 70% took knives) — even in this scenario, there would still be a substantial net increase in homicides according to one study. This is because long guns are inherently more accurate and devastating. They are much more likely to kill someone than a handgun.

If only cheap handguns were banned, meanwhile, the result would be the same. Criminals would shift to larger caliber handguns which are intrinsically more accurate. That means more deaths from assaults.

And what if the impossible came about, what if every criminal decided to change to knives instead of guns? Even in this fairy-tale scenario, the results wouldn't be nearly as nice as the gun banners imply. For according to some studies, guns are only slightly more devastating than knives. One study in 1977, for example, found guns to be only 1.31 times more deadly than knives in assaults during robberies.

["Firearms and Firearms Regulation: Old Premises, New Research," pp. 278-280]

Semi-Automatic "Assault Rifles"

Semi-automatic weapon technology has existed since the turn of the century. Recently, however, the gun grabbers have seized upon a single tragedy to begin a movement to ban these weapons which are owned by 20—30 million Americans. They have based their case on distortions and outright lies in their enormously successful campaign against "assault rifles."

The "Assault Rifle" Facts

For starters, an "assault rifle," according to the Department of Defense, is a weapon that can fire multiple rounds with each trigger pull (commonly known as a machine gun). These fully-automatic weapons have been under strict government control since 1934 (National Firearms Act). No legally registered fully-automatic has ever been used in a crime. Of course, criminals still use automatic weapons, but, as I have often said, criminals don't register their guns.

The so-called "assault rifles" that the gun grabbers want to ban require a pull and release of the trigger to fire each round. That means that a so-called "assault rifle" fires no faster than a revolver or a slide-operated firearm.

The media, aiding the gun grabbers, often distort the issue by showing a fully-automatic weapon being fired while talking about bills to restrict "assault rifles." Although some semi-automatic rifles *look* like fully-automatic weapons, any similarity is purely cosmetic.

The anti-gunners claim that semi-automatic weapons can easily be converted to "machine guns," but the facts deny that this is the case. According to Los Angeles Police Detective Jimmy Trahin, "this media blitz of many of these military-style weapons being converted is not true."

149

The gun grabbers themselves don't know what weapons they want to ban. In a recent debate with Michael Beard of the National Coalition to Ban Handguns (and now semi-automatic weapons), he was asked to define an "assault rifle." He said he couldn't. At least he's honest—uninformed, but honest.

Although the ads run by the anti-gunners feature weapons that look sinister and fully automatic, almost every definition of "assault rifle" that they have come up with includes most semi-automatic hunting rifles and handguns.

The Uzi and MAC-10 pistol, both mentioned as "assault rifles," actually fire handgun bullets. That is the danger of allowing the anti-gunners to make firearms policy. When it comes to guns, they don't know a Daisy from a Ruger.

The main argument against "assault rifles"—that their only purpose is to kill a human being—is completely fallacious. The so-called "assault rifle" is actually designed to wound rather than kill. The reason for this is that in war time it is better to wound the enemy than kill him since a wounded man, besides being incapacitated, has to be treated and protected, which imposes a continuing burden on the opposition.

The "assault rifle" itself fires a lighter cartridge than many hunting rifles and some pistols. It is fortunate that Patrick Purdy used an AK-47 rather than a high caliber weapon in the Stockton massacre. Otherwise, 30 of the 35 hit would probably not have survived.

In fact, despite claims that semi-automatic weapons are "the weapons of choice for gang members and drug dealers," less than 3% of the weapons confiscated in Los Angeles fall in the class of "military-style semi-automatics." Only 4% of homicides nation-wide involve *any* type of rifle—military style or not.

According to the BATF, only 1% of military-style semi-automatics are misused. Isn't it just like the gun grabbers to punish the other 99% of us instead?

The Constitution and "Assault Rifles"

Perhaps the best argument for keeping "assault rifles" in the hands of law-abiding citizens was provided by the gun grabbers themselves. Back when the gun grabbers wanted to ban Saturday Night Specials (they still do, their focus has just shifted), they argued that such a ban would be constitutional because Saturday Night Specials have no use in a militia—in other words, they are not military weapons.

Now they argue that "assault rifles" should be banned because they have *only* military uses. Just how consistent is that? First they want to ban our guns because they *can't* be used for military purposes and now they want to ban them because they *can*. (Could it be that they want *all* our guns?)

The truth is that, by their own definitions, a ban on "assault rifles" would be unconstitutional since these are the very weapons that would be used by a militia. Finally the gun grabbers and I agree on something!

The Supreme Court agrees as well.   In the 1939 case *U. S.* v. *Miller,* the Supreme Court ruled that only weapons that are "part of the ordinary military equipment or that . . . could contribute to the common defense" were protected by the Second Amendment.

Protection From Tyranny

The reason the Founding Fathers wrote the Second Amendment to protect firearms like "assault rifles" is so Americans would have the ability to resist a tyrannical government should one try to take control. Although the possibility of a foreign invasion or domestic attempt to take over the government seems remote today, it is impossible to judge what the political situation will be in the year 2000 and beyond.

Remember, it took Adolf Hitler only fourteen years to take control of Germany, and only one month to conquer France, a major European power. Here's what Hitler had to say about gun control: "The most foolish mistake we could possibly make would be to allow the subject races to possess arms."

If a Hitler ever came to power in America, I would much rather have an "assault rifle" than a membership card for Handgun Control, Inc. George Washington would have agreed. Said he: "[Firearms] are the American people's liberty teeth and keystone under independence. . . . The very atmosphere of firearms everywhere restrains evil interference—they deserve a place of honor with all that's good."

Personally, I'd rather America followed the path of a man who refused a monarchy and created a democracy than one who destroyed a democracy and created a fascist state, but Handgun Control, Inc. has other ideas.

Questions and Answers About Semi-Automatics

Q? What is the difference between an "Assault Rifle" and a semi-automatic sporting rifle?

A: According to the Department of Defense, assault rifles are short, compact, selective-fire weapons that, at the operator's discretion, can fire automatically or semi-automatically. A full-automatic firearm (machine gun) will fire a continuous burst of ammunition as long as the trigger is being depressed. Semi-automatic firearms fire one round of ammunition for each pull of the trigger and do not have full-automatic fire capability.

Q? Are semi-automatic sporting rifles easily convertible to full-automatic?

A: No. In testimony before the California State Assembly, Los Angeles Police Detective Jimmy Trahin, who is the firearms expert for the L.A.P.D., stated, "These military style assault weapons of today are not easily and readily convertible without extensive knowledge and modifications to the weapon and or substitution of available parts."

Q? Are semi-automatic rifles being converted by criminals to full-automatic (machine gun)?

A: No. In the last 12 years the L.A.P.D. firearms squad has taken into custody over 50,000 firearms and has never had any semi-automatic AK-47s, semi-automatic H&K 91s, semi-automatic H&K 93s or semi-automatic Ruger Mini 14 converted and a few unsuccessful attempts to covert semi-automatic AR-15s to full-automatic by substituting M-16 parts. Each year they handle over 4,000 firearms of which an average of 12 (.003 percent) have had conversions. Of those converted firearms, less than half were operational.

Q? Are these semi-automatic military rifles more deadly than semi-automatic hunting rifles?

A: No. In fact, the opposite is true. According to Dr. Martin L. Fackler, Director of the Wound Ballistics Laboratory at the Letterman Army Institute of Research at the Presidio of San Francisco: "The full-metal-jacketed military bullets designed for use in 'assault rifles' are specifically made so as to limit tissue disruption, i.e., to wound rather than to kill . . . . By the same token, military bullets are prohibited for hunting because they lack tissue disruption capacity—they are more likely to wound than to kill."

Q? Why are semi-automatic versions of military style "assault rifles" under such attack?

A: Most proponents of handgun control have accepted as fact the inability of the handgun restriction movement to organize itself into an effective electoral threat. They have found marginal success by attacking such firearms issues as armor piercing ammunition, plastic guns, and machine guns. These were *new* topics! So is the "assault rifle" issue. They suspect that by coupling the menacing looks of an assault rifle with the public's confusion over semi-automatic and full-automatic firearms they can increase the chances for restrictions of these types of firearms. In other words, if it's black and looks bad, it must be evil. A win for the pro-control advocates on this issue will surely pave they way for additional bans on other, if not all, firearms.

Q? Are semi-automatic sporting arms a crime problem in the United States?

A: No, according to Stephen E. Higgins, Director of the Bureau of Alcohol, Tobacco and Firearms in statements made on March 15, 1989, 10% of the firearms used in violent crime are semi-automatic pistols and rifles. Less than 1% are semi-automatic military type firearms.

Q? Are semi-automatic sporting rifles the weapon of choice of today's drug dealers as portrayed by the anti-gunners and the media?

A: No.

> **Fact:** George Wilson, head of the Firearms Examination Division of the Washington, D. C., Police force, stated, "In 1988 the department had not recovered any of the rifles covered by last month's importation ban." (March 14, 1989 importation moratorium imposed by Drug Czar William Bennett pending a BATF study.)

> **Fact:** City of Seattle police have not had a homicide involving a semi-automatic sporting rifle of the type referred to by the media as an "assault rifle" in the past 5 years. (April 1989.)

> **Fact:** Of 14,988 guns seized by the Chicago police in 1988, 11,263 were revolvers and pistols and 469 were semi-automatic rifles. Of the semi-automatic rifles seized, no distinction was made between military style and those of sporting design.

> **Fact:** New York City Police Lt. James Moran told

the *New York Times* (Feb. 5, 1989) that hardly any of the 16,370 weapons seized in 1988 were assault rifles, which he described as "cumbersome" and unpopular with drug dealers, who prefer concealable handguns.

Q? Does the nation's law enforcement community favor a ban on semi-automatic sporting rifles as portrayed by the media and the anti-gun groups?

A: No. Contrary to comments by a few elitist police chiefs, the majority of the nation's top police officers are opposed to such bans. The "1989 Law Enforcement Officers' Poll" of 16,000 police chiefs and sheriffs conducted by the National Association of Chiefs of Police shows that 71% support the right of law abiding citizens to purchase ANY type of firearm while 88% do not believe that a ban of "military type" long rifles will reduce criminal acquisition of them.

Section III
References

Radio Show Fact Sheet: The Myths of Gun Control

Myth #1:   Gun control is progressive

Fact: Some of the first American gun control laws were those enacted to keep Southern blacks defenseless and in subjugation. Before the Civil War, slave codes barred both slaves and free blacks from owning arms — except under extremely narrow circumstances. After the war, the slave codes reappeared as "black codes." Once again, the right of arms was denied to blacks. Congress was so enraged that it passed the 15th Amendment to nullify such statutes. Southern states then ingeniously circumvented the Amendment by banning all but the most expensive handguns — thus placing handgun ownership out of the average black's reach. [Stephen Halbrook, Ph.D., J.D., has taught legal philosophy and political philosophy at George Mason University]

Fact: At the turn of the century, gun control in the north was spurred by anti-immigrant hysteria. Under New York's Sullivan Law, for example, Southern and Eastern European immigrants found it virtually impossible to legally own guns — because the police would rarely issue them permits. [William Tonso, sociology professor at University of Evansville (Indiana)]

Fact: Today, proposals to ban "Saturday Night Specials" are merely a rehash of the black codes in the South. Cheap handguns allow poverty stricken blacks and whites a chance to defend themselves. Ban cheap handguns and only the rich will be able to afford protection.

Myth #2: Areas with strict gun control have lower crime rates/area with loose controls have higher crime rates.

Fact: In 1966, New Jersey passed a gun control law described by its sponsors as "the most stringent" in America. In the 5 years after it went into effect, murders rose 65.7%, rape rose 55.9%, and robbery jumped a staggering 245%.

Fact: In 1967, Hawaii enacted a tough gun law. In the five years following, robbery was up 180%, murder was up 183%, and rape skyrocketed 326%!

Fact: Twenty percent of all homicides in this country occur in 4 cities with just 6% of the population — New York, Chicago, Detroit and Washington, D.C. All have strict gun control.

Fact: In 1974, Jamaica outlawed the private ownership of all firearms and ammunition. Possession of a single bullet was made punishable by life in prison. Six years later, Jamaica had 6 times as many gun deaths per capita as Washington, D.C. — one of the most violent cities in America.

Fact: The four countries with the highest gun ownership rates all have low crime rates. These countries are Switzerland, Israel, Denmark and Finland.

Myth #3: **Handguns are responsible for many accidents and suicides — Gun Control will prevent these.**

Fact: Accidental gun deaths account for only about 2% of all accidental deaths. Further, over 99.9% of all households with a handgun do not experience a fatal firearms accident during the year. [Sociologists Peter Rossi and James Wright]

Fact: During 1982, you were 26 times more likely to die in a car accident than from a gun accident. You were almost 7 times more likely to die by falling down. You were nearly 2 times more likely to die by drowning. And you were about 2.7 times more likely to die by being poisoned.

Fact: Among men, about 36% of suicides are done by methods other than firearms. Among women, about 59% of suicides are done by methods other than firearms. These statistics demonstrate that there are many other ways to kill one's self besides using a gun. So banning guns will hardly stop suicides. People will simply use other methods.

Fact: Tough gun laws don't guarantee lower suicide rates. Japan and Sweden both have tough anti-gun laws. Both have higher suicide rates than those here in the U.S. Japan's suicide rate in 1982 was 34.4 people per 100,000; Sweden's was 35.2 per 100,000. The U.S.'s suicide rate, by comparison, was roughly 1/3 — 23.7 per 100,000.

Fact: High gun ownership rates don't guarantee high suicide rates. Israel has one of the highest gun ownership rates in the world. Yet in 1982 its suicide rate was only 11.9 per 100,000 — less than the rates in countries with strict gun laws like Japan, Sweden and Britain. [The statistics cited in this section, unless otherwise noted, come from the Statistical Abstract of the United

States: 1986, U.S. Bureau of the Census, Washington, D.C., 1985]

Myth #4: Gun Control will stop crimes of passion.

Fact: Most family killings are not committed by "normal" people who, in a burst of anger, pull the trigger on their spouse or child. According to FBI figures, over two-thirds of those homicide offenders arrested between 1970 and 1975 had prior arrest records. According to a computer study done for the Eisenhower Commission, it was further determined that nearly 75% of those arrested between 1964 and 1967 for homicides had a record of previous arrests for "a major violent crime or burglary." In other words, the average perpetrator of a crime of passion is a violent sociopath — just the type of person least likely to obey gun laws.

Myth #5: A handgun is a poor defensive weapon.

Fact: A study of Chicago robberies done during the 1970's showed that handguns were far superior to six other self-defense methods. Those who used handguns were able to foil the robbery and keep their property in two-thirds of the studied incidents. Those who used a non-gun weapon were successful in only 40% of the incidents. Those using physical force were successful in only 22% of the incidents. Those who used verbal shouts ere successful in only 20% of the incidents.

Fact: According to a poll conducted in 1978, 13 million registered voters live in households where a family member has had to use a gun in self-defense. According to the same poll, over five million voters or their families had actually fired a gun for self-protection. [Decision Making Information Poll]

Fact: A 1978 Cadell Poll for Milton Eisenhower's Center for the Study of Handgun Violence projected that 300,000 Americans use a handgun each year to deter crime.

Myth #6: The Second Amendment doesn't guarantee an individual right to keep and bear arms.

Fact: The Second Amendment itself is clear. "A well-regulated militia being necessary to the security of a free state, the right of the people to keep and bear arms shall not be infringed."

Fact: The word 'militia' does not refer to a group like the National Guard. The Founding Fathers were clear that the militia was the whole citizenry. Patrick Henry said in 1782: "Who are the militia? They consist now of the whole people." The Militia Act of 1792 defined the militia as including "every, free, white, able-bodied male." And the current U.S. Code, Title 10, section 31 says that the militia of each state includes "all able-bodied males at least 17 years of age and ... under 45 years of age who are, or have made declaration of intention to become, citizens."

Myth #7: The majority of Americans want gun control.

The evidence on gun control and public opinion is contradictory — largely reflecting what types of questions are asked. When people are asked merely whether they favor "gun control," they usually respond in the affirmative.

BUT an even greater majority of the people ALSO support the right to own guns.

Fact: According to polls, 89% of Americans believe that they have a right to own a gun.

- 87% of the people believe that the U.S. Constitution gives them the right to keep and bear arms.

- 91% of the people agree that registration of handguns will not prevent criminals from acquiring or using them for illegal purposes. [Decision Making Information polls]

- 58% of the people disagree that we should ban the future manufacture and sale of all handguns. [Cadell poll]

Fact: Voters have consistently rejected strict gun control measures across the nation — by 2 to 1 in Massachusetts in 1976, and by 63% in California in 1982.

Reference Resources

Those materials with a star can be purchased from the Second Amendment Foundation. Write the Foundation at 12500 N.E. Tenth Place, Bellevue, WA 98005 and request a price list. Or call the Foundation at (206) 454-7012.

* Armed and Alive, by Massad F. Ayoob, Second Amendment Monograph Series (Second Amendment Foundation, Bellevue, WA: 1982)

* The Battle Over Gun Control, by Don B. Kates, Jr., Second Amendment Foundation Monograph Series (Second Amendment Foundation, Bellevue, WA: 1986)

* The BATF's War on Civil Liberties: The Assault on Gun Owners, Report of the Task Force to Investigate the Enforcement Policies of the Bureau of Alcohol, Tobacco and Firearms (Second Amendment Foundation, Bellevue, WA: 1979)

* Calling the Shots, by William R. Tonso, Second Amendment Foundation Monograph Series (Second Amendment Foundation, Bellevue, WA: 1985)

* The Case Against Gun Control, by Jeffrey Kane, Second Amendment Foundation Monograph Series (Second Amendment Foundation, Bellevue, WA: 1976)

Crime by Choice: An Economic Analysis, by Morgan O. Reynolds (Fisher Institute, Dallas, TX: 1984)

* Do Police Support Gun Control? The Definitive Survey, Second Amendment Foundation Monograph Series (Second Amendment Foundation, Bellevue, WA: 1986)

That Every Man Be Armed: The Evolution of a Constitutional Right, by Stephen Halbrook (University of New Mexico Press, Albuquerque: 1984)

* "Firearms and Firearms Regulation: Old Premises, New Research," collection of essays, ed. by Don. Kates, Jr., in Law and Policy Quarterly: An Interdisciplinary Journal, July 1983 (Sage Publications, Beverly Hills, CA)

* Firearms and Violence: Issues of Public Policy, ed. by Don Kates, Jr. (Pacific Institute for Public Policy Research, San Fransisco: 1984; published by Ballinger Publishing Company, Cambridge, Massachusetts, a subsidiary of Harper and Row)

* In the Gravest Extreme: The Role of the Firearm in Personal Protection, by Massad F. Ayoob (Massad and Dorothy Ayoob, Publisher: 1980)

Gun Control, by Robert J. Kukla (Stackpole Books, Harrisburg, PA: 1973)

Gun Control and National Magazine Media, by Gary B. Bullert (Second Amendment Foundation, Bellevue, WA: 1985)

* Gun Control: White Man's Law, by William R. Tonso (Second Amendment Foundation, Bellevue, WA: 1985)

* The Gun Grabbers, by Alan Gottlieb (Merril Press, Bellevue, WA: 1986)

Gun Week, the most comprehensive weekly publication for gun activists. Subscriptions: $20.00/one year, U.S. (Can be ordered from Second Amendment Foundation, P.O. Box 488, Station C, Buffalo, NY 14209)

* Handgun Prohibition and the Original Meaning of the Second Amendment, by Don Kates, Jr., Second Amendment Foundation Monograph Series (Second Amendment Foundation, Bellevue, WA: 1984)

Myths About Guns, by James Edwards (Peninsula Press, Coral Springs, FL: 1978)

* The Police View of Gun Control, by Massad F. Ayoob, Second Amendment Foundation Monograph Series (Second Amendment Foundation, Bellevue, WA 1981)

* Restricting Handguns: The Liberal Skeptics Speak Out, ed. by Don Kates, Jr. (North River Press, Inc: 1979)

* The Rights of Gun Owners, by Alan Gottlieb, a Second Amendment Foundation Handbook (Green Hill Publishers, Inc., Ottawa, Illinois: 1983)

* The Second Amendment: Second to None, by Don B. Kates, Jr., Second Amendment Foundation Monograph Series (Second Amendment Foundation, Bellevue, WA: 1982)

Sourcebook of Criminal Justice Statistics — 1985, edited by Timothy J. Flanagan and Edmund F. McGarrell (U.S. Department of Justice, Bureau of Justice Statistics: 1984)

Statistical Abstract of the United States — 1987 (U.S. Bureau of the Census: 1986)

Under the Gun: Weapons, Crime, and Violence in America, by James D. Wright, Peter H. Rossi, and Kathleen Daly (Aldine Publishing Co., New York: 1983)

Women's Views on Guns and Self-Defense, Second Amendment Foundation Monograph Series (Second Amendment Foundation, Bellevue, WA: 1983)

NOTES

NOTES